THREE COMEDIES BY BJÖRNSON: TRANSLATED BY R. FARQUHARSON SHARP

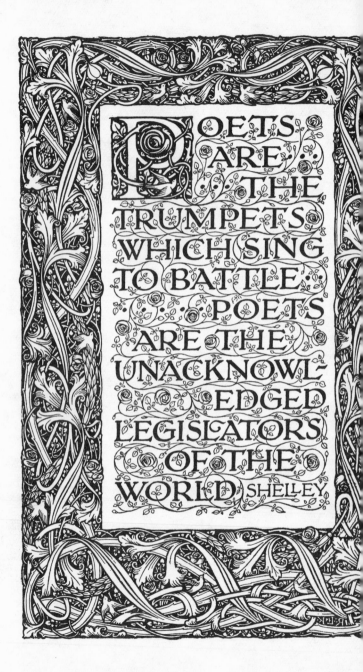

POETS ARE THE TRUMPETS WHICH SING TO BATTLE · POETS ARE THE UNACKNOWLEDGED LEGISLATORS OF THE WORLD · SHELLEY

ℭℭ THREE COMEDIES by BJÖRNSTJERNE BJÖRNSON

GREENWOOD PRESS, PUBLISHERS
WESTPORT, CONNECTICUT

Library of Congress Cataloging in Publication Data

Bjørnson, Bjørnstjerne, 1832–1910.
   Three comedies.

   Translated by R. F. Sharp.
   Reprint of the ed. originally published in 1912
by J. M. Dent, London, in series: Everyman's library;
poetry and rama, no. 625.
   CONTENTS: The newly-married couple.—Leonarda.—
A gauntlet.
PT8816.A3S5 1974b   839.8'2'26   73-17652
ISBN 0-8371-7259-4

Originally published in 1912 by J.M. Dent & Sons Ltd, London;
E.P. Dutton & Co., New York

Reprinted in 1974 by Greenwood Press,
a division of Williamhouse-Regency Inc.

Library of Congress Catalog Card Number 73-17652

ISBN 0-8371-7259-4

Printed in the United States of America

INTRODUCTION

BJÖRNSTJERNE BJÖRNSON—poet, dramatist, novelist, and politician, and the most notable figure in contemporary Norwegian history—was born, in December 1832, at Kvikne in the north of Norway. His father was pastor at Kvikne, a remote village in the Österdal district, some sixty miles south of Trondhjem; a lonely spot, whose atmosphere and surroundings Björnson afterwards described in one of his short sketches ("Blakken"). The pastor's house lay so high up on the "fjeld" that corn would not grow on its meadows, where the relentless northern winter seemed to begin so early and end so late. The Österdal folk were a wild, turbulent lot in those days—so much so, that his predecessor (who had never ventured into the church without his pistol in his pocket) had eventually run away and flatly refused to return, with the result that the district was pastorless for some years until the elder Björnson came to it.

It was in surroundings such as this, and with scarcely any playfellows, that Björnstjerne Björnson spent the first six years of his life; and the sturdy independence of his nature may have owed something to the unaccommodating life of his earliest days, just as the poetical impulse that was so strong in his developed character probably had its beginnings in the impressions of beauty he received in the years that immediately followed. For, when he was six, a welcome change came. His father was transferred to the tranquil pastorate of Naes, at the mouth of the Romsdal, one of the fairest spots in Norway. Here Björnson spent the rest of his childhood, in surroundings of beauty and peacefulness, going to school first at Molde and afterwards at Christiania, to pass on later to the Christiania

University where he graduated in 1852. As a boy, his earliest biographer tells us, he was fully determined to be a poet—and, naturally, the foremost poet of his time!—but, as years passed, he gained a soberer estimate of his possibilities. At the University he was one of a group of kindred spirits with eager literary leanings, and it did not take him long to gain a certain footing in the world of journalism. His work for the first year or two was mainly in the domain of dramatic criticism, but the creative instinct was growing in him. A youthful effort of his—a drama entitled *Valborg*—was actually accepted for production at the Christiania theatre, and the author, according to custom, was put on the " free list " at once. The experience he gained, however, by assiduous attendance at the theatre so convinced him of the defects in his own bantling, that he withdrew it before performance—a heroic act of self-criticism rare amongst young authors.

His first serious literary efforts were some peasant tales, whose freshness and vividness made an immediate and remarkable impression and practically ensured his future as a writer, while their success inspired him with the desire to create a kind of peasant " saga." He wrote of what he knew, and a delicate sense of style seemed inborn in him. The best known of these tales are *Synnöve Solbakken* (1857) and *Arne* (1858). They were hailed as giving a revelation of the Norwegian character, and the first-named was translated into English as early as 1858. He was thus made known to (or, at any rate, accessible to) English readers many years before Ibsen, though his renown was subsequently overshadowed, out of their own country, by the enormous vogue of the latter's works. Ibsen, too, has been far more widely translated (and is easier to translate) into English than Björnson. Much of the latter's finest work, especially in his lyrical poetry and his peasant stories, has a charm of diction that it is almost impossible to reproduce in translation. Ibsen and Björnson, who inevitably suggest comparison when either's work is dealt with, were closely bound by friendship as well as admiration until a breach was caused by Björnson's taking offence at a supposed attack on him in Ibsen's early play *The League of Youth*, Björnson considering himself to be lampooned in the delineation of one of the characters thereof. The breach, however, was healed many years later, when, at the time of the bitter attacks that were made upon Ibsen in consequence of the publication of *Ghosts*, Björnson came into the field of controversy with a vigorous and generous championing of his rival.

Björnson's dramatic energies, as was the case with Ibsen in his early days, first took the form of a series of historical dramas—*Sigurd Slembe*, *Konge Sverre*, and others; and he was intimately connected with the theatre by being for two periods theatrical director, from 1857 to 1859 at Bergen and from 1865 to 1867 at Christiania. Previous to the latter engagement a stipend granted to him by the Norwegian government enabled him to travel for two or three years in Europe; and during those years his pen was never idle—poems, prose sketches, and tales flowing from it in abundance. *De Nygifte* (*The Newly-Married Couple*), the first of the three plays in the present volume, was produced at the Christiania theatre in the first year of his directorship there.

The two volumes, *Digte og Sange* (*Poems and Songs*) and *Arnljot Gelline*, which comprise the greater proportion of Björnson's poetry, both appeared in 1870. *Digte og Sange* was republished, in an enlarged edition, ten years later. It contains the poem " Ja, vi elsker dette Landet " (" Yes, we love this land of ours "), which, set to inspiring music by Nordraak, became Norway's most favourite national song, as well as another of the same nature—" Fremad! Fremad! " (" Forward! Forward! ")—which, sung to music of Grieg's, ran it hard in popularity. Of " Ja, vi elsker dette Landet," Björnson used to say that the greatest tribute he had ever had to its hold upon his fellow-countrymen's hearts was when, on one occasion during the poet's years of vigorous political activity, a crowd of fervid

opponents came and broke his windows with stones;
after which, turning to march away triumphantly, they
felt the need (ever present to the Scandinavian in
moments of stress) of singing, and burst out with one
accord into the " Ja, vi elsker dette Landet " of their
hated political adversary.   " They couldn't help it;
they had to sing it! " the poet used to relate delightedly.

Of the birth of " Fremad! Fremad! " Grieg has left
an account which gives an amusing picture of the
infectious enthusiasm that was one of Björnson's
strongest characteristics.   Grieg had given him, as a
Christmas present, the first series of his " Lyrical
Pieces " for the pianoforte, and had afterwards played
some of them to the poet, who was especially struck
with one melody which Grieg had called " Fädrelands-
sang " (" Song of the Fatherland ").   Björnson there
and then, to the composer's great gratification, protested
that he must write words to fit the air.   (It must be
mentioned that each strophe of the melody starts with
a refrain consisting of two strongly accented notes,
which suggest some vigorous dissyllabic word.)   A day
or two later Grieg met Björnson, who was in the full
throes of composition, and exclaimed to him that the
song was going splendidly, and that he believed all the
youth of Norway would adopt it enthusiastically; but
that he was still puzzled over the very necessary word
to fit the strongly marked refrain.   However, he was
not going to give it up.   Next morning, when Grieg was
in his room peacefully giving a piano lesson to a young
lady, a furious ringing was heard at his front-door bell,
as if the ringer would tear the bell from its wires,
followed by a wild shout of " ' Fremad! Fremad! '
Hurrah, I have got it! ' Fremad! ' " Björnson, for
of course the intruder was he, rushed into the house
the moment the maid's trembling fingers could open the
door, and triumphantly chanted the completed song to
them, over and over again, amidst a din of laughter and
congratulations.

His first experiments in the " social drama," plays
dealing with the tragedies and comedies of every-day

life in his own country, were made at about the same time as Ibsen's; that is to say, in the seventies. Björnson's first successes in that field, which made him at once a popular dramatist, were *Redaktören* (*The Editor*) in 1874 and *En Fallit* (*A Bankruptcy*) in 1875. The latter especially was hailed as the earliest raising of the veil upon Norwegian domestic life, and as a remarkable effort in the detection of drama in the commonplace. Before he wrote these, Björnson had again been for some years out of Norway; and, as in the case of Ibsen, who began the writing of his " social dramas " when in voluntary exile, absence seemed to enable him to observe the familiar from a new stand-point and in the proper perspective.

After his first successes in this line, when his plays (and his poems and tales to an equal extent) had made him popular and honoured among his own people, Björnson settled at Aulestad, which remained his home for the rest of his life. He also became a doughty controversialist in social and religious matters, and the first outcome of this phase was his play *Leonarda* (the second in this volume), which was first performed in 1879, to be followed by *Det ny System* (*The New System*) later in the same year. These works aroused keen controversy, but were not such popular stage successes as his earlier plays. Moreover, about this time, on his return from a visit to America, he plunged into the vortex of political controversy as an aggressive radical. He was a vigorous and very persuasive orator; and in that capacity, as well as in that of writer of political articles and essays, was an uncompromising foe to the opportunist theories which he held to be degrading the public life of his country. The opposition he aroused by his fearless championship of whatever he considered a rightful cause was so bitter that he was eventually obliged to retire from Norway for two or three years. So much did this temporarily affect his literary reputation at home, that when, in 1883, he had written *En Hanske* (*A Gauntlet*—the third play here translated) he found at first considerable difficulty in getting it

performed. Later, however, he became a political hero
to a large section of his compatriots, and by degrees
won back fully the place he had occupied in their hearts.
He enthusiastically espoused the cause of the projected
separation from Sweden, though when that matter came
to a crisis he exercised an invaluable influence on the
side of moderation.

For the remainder of his life he continued to be
prolific in literary production, with an ever increasing
renown amongst European men of letters, and an ever
deepening personal hold upon the affections of his
fellow-countrymen. In 1903 he was awarded the Nobel
prize for literature. During his later years he, like
Ibsen, was a determined opponent of the movement
to replace the Dano-Norwegian language, which had
hitherto been the literary vehicle of Norwegian writers,
by the " Bonde-Maal " — or " Ny Norsk " (" New
Norwegian "), as it has lately been termed. This is
an artificial hybrid composed from the Norwegian
peasant dialects, by the use of which certain misguided
patriots were (and unfortunately still are) anxious to
dissociate their literature from that of Denmark.
Björnson, and with him most of the soberer spirits
amongst Norwegian writers, had realised that the
door which had so long shut out Norway from the
literature of Europe must be, as he put it, opened from
the inside; and he rightly considered that the ill-
judged " Bonde-Maal " movement could only have the
result of wedging the door more tightly shut.

He died, in April 1910, in Paris, where for some years
he had always spent his winters, and was buried at
home with every mark of honour and regret, a Norwegian
warship having been sent to convey his remains back
to his own land.

He was a man of very lovable personality and of the
kindest heart; easily moved by any tale of oppression
or injustice, and of wide-armed (albeit sometimes in-
judicious) generosity; more apt, in the affairs of every-
day life, to be governed by his heart than by his head,
and as simple as a child in many matters. His wife was

an ideal helpmate to him, and their family life very happy.

The Newly-Married Couple (1865) offers a considerable contrast to the other two plays here presented. It belongs to the school of Scribe and the " soliloquy," and the author avails himself of the recognised dramatic conventions of the day. At the same time, though the characters may be conventional in type, they are, thanks to Björnson's sense of humour, alive; and the theme of the estrangement and reconciliation of the " newly-married couple " is treated with delicacy and charm. It is true that it is almost unbelievable that the hero could be so stupid as to allow the " confidante " to accompany his young wife when he at last succeeds in wresting her from her parents' jealous clutches; but, on the other hand, that lady, with her anonymous novel that revealed the truth to the young couple, was necessary to the plot as a " dea ex machina." The play was, and is, immensely popular on the Scandinavian stage, and still holds the boards on others. It has been translated into Swedish, German, English, Dutch, Italian, Polish and Finnish.

Leonarda (1879) marks just as striking an advance upon Björnson's early plays as the first of Ibsen's " social dramas " did upon his. Unreal stage conventions have disappeared, the characterisation is convincing, and the dialogue, if more prolix than Ibsen's (as is throughout the case with Björnson), is always interesting and individual. The emotional theme of the play, the love of an older woman for her adopted daughter's young lover, is treated with the poetic touch that pervades all Björnson's work; and the controversial theme, that of religious tolerance, with a sane restraint. It cannot be denied, however, that Björnson's changed and unorthodox attitude towards religious matters—an attitude little expected except by those who knew him best—contributed a good deal towards the temporary waning of his popularity at this time. *Leonarda* is (like *A Gauntlet*) a good example of the root difference between Björnson's and

Ibsen's treatment of problems in their dramas. Ibsen contented himself with diagnosing social maladies; Björnson's more genial nature hints also at the remedy, or at least at a palliative. Ibsen is a stern judge; Björnson is, beyond that, a prophet of better things. Whereas Ibsen is first and foremost a dramatist, Björnson is rather by instinct the novelist who casts his ideas in dramatic form, and is concerned to " round up " the whole. As Brandes says, in the course of his sympathetic criticism of the two writers, " Ibsen is in love with the idea, and its psychological and logical consequences. . . . Corresponding to this love of the abstract idea in Ibsen, we have in Björnson the love of humankind." Björnson, moreover, was a long way behind Ibsen in constructive skill. As regards the technical execution of *Leonarda*, its only obvious weakness is a slight want of vividness in the presentation of the thesis. The hiatuses between the acts leave perhaps too much to the imagination, and the play needs more than a cursory reading for us to grasp the full import of the actions and motives of its personages. *Leonarda* has not been previously translated into English; though Swedish, French, German and Finnish versions of it exist.

A Gauntlet (finished in 1883) shows a great advance in dramatic technique. The whole is closely knit and coherent, and the problems involved are treated with an exhaustiveness that is equally fair to both sides. As has been already said, the plays that had preceded it from Björnson's pen aroused such active controversy that he found it at first impossible to get *A Gauntlet* produced in his own country. Its first performance was in Hamburg, in 1883, and for that the author modified and altered it greatly. Eventually it was played, in its original form, in the Scandinavian countries, and in its turn stirred up a bitter controversy on the ethics of male and female morality as regards marriage. It was currently said that hundreds of contemplated marriages were broken off in Norway as an effect of its statement of a vital problem. The remodelling the play originally

underwent for its performance in Germany was drastic.
The second and third acts were entirely recast, the
character of Dr. Nordan was omitted and others introduced, and the ending was changed. The first version
was, however, evidently the author's favourite, and it
is that that is presented here. Björnson never published
the recast version, and in the "memorial edition" of
his works it is the present version that is given. The
recast version was translated into English by Mr.
Osman Edwards and produced (in an "adapted" and
mangled form, for which the translator was not responsible) at the Royalty Theatre in London in 1894.

R. FARQUHARSON SHARP.

BIBLIOGRAPHY

DRAMATIC AND POETIC WORKS.—Mellem Slagene (Between the
Battles), 1857. Halte-Hulda (Lame Hulda), 1858. Kong Sverre
(King Sverre), 1861. Sigurd Slembe (Sigurd the Bastard), 1862;
translated by W. M. Payne, 1888. Maria Stuart i Skotland, 1864.
De Nygifte (The Newly-Married Couple), 1865; translated by
T. Soelfeldt, 1868; by S. and E. Hjerleid, 1870; as A Lesson in
Marriage, by G. I. Colbron, 1911. Sigurd Jorsalfar (Sigurd the
Crusader), 1872. Redaktören (The Editor), 1874. En Fallit (A
Bankruptcy), 1874. Kongen (The King), 1877. Leonarda, 1879.
Det ny System (The New System), 1879. En Hanske, 1883; trans-
lated as A Gauntlet, by H. L. Bræmstad, 1890; by Osman Edwards,
1894. Over Ævne (Beyond our Strength), Part I., 1883; translated
as Pastor Sang, by W. Wilson, 1893; Part II., 1895. Geografi og
Kærlighed (Geography and Love), 1885; Paul Lange og Tora
Parsberg, 1898; translated by H. L. Bræstad, 1899. Laboremus,
1901; translation published by Chapman and Hall, 1901. Paa
Storhove (At Storhove), 1904; Daglannet, 1904; Naar den ny Vin
blomstrer (When the Vineyards are in Blossom), 1909.
   Digte og Sange (Poems and Songs), 1870; Arnljot Gelline, 1870.

FICTION.—Synnöve Solbakken, 1857; translated as Trust and
Trial, by Mary Howitt, 1858; as Love and Life in Norway, by Hon.
Augusta Bethell and A. Plesner, 1870; as The Betrothal, in H. and
A. Zimmern's Half-hours with Foreign Novelists, 1880; also translated by Julie Sutter, 1881; by R. B. Anderson, 1881. Arne, 1858;
translated by T. Krag, 1861; by A. Plesner and S. Rugeley-Powers,
1866; by R. B. Anderson, 1881; by W. Low (Bohn's Library),
1890. Smaastykker (Sketches), 1860. En glad Gut, 1860; translated as Ovind, by S. and E. Hjerleid, 1869; as The Happy Boy,
by R. B. Anderson, 1881; as The Happy Lad (published by Blackie),

1882. Fiskerjenten, 1868; translated as The Fisher Maiden, by M. E. Niles, 1869; as The Fishing Girl, by A. Plesner and F. Richardson, 1870; as The Fishing Girl, by S. and E. Hjerleid, 1871; as The Fisher Maiden, by R. B. Anderson, 1882. Brude-Slaatten, 1873; translated as The Bridal March, by R. B. Anderson, 1882; by J. E. Williams, 1893. Fortællinger (Tales), 1872. Magnhild, 1877; translated by R. B. Anderson, 1883. Kaptejn Mansana, 1879; translated as Captain Mansana by R. B. Anderson, 1882. Det flager i Byen og paa Havnen (Flags are Flying in Town and Port), 1884; translated as The Heritage of the Kurts, by C Fairfax, 1892. Paa Guds Veje, 1889; translated as In God's Way, by E. Carmichael, 1890. Nye Fortællinger (New Tales), 1894; To Fortællinger (Two Tales), 1901; Mary, 1906. Collected edition of the Novels, translated into English, edited by E. Gosse, 13 vols., 1895-1909.

[*See* Life of Björnson by W. M. Payne, 1910; E. Gosse's Study of the Writings of Björnson, in edition of Novels, 1895; H. H. Boyesen's Essays on Scandinavian Literature, 1895; G. Brandes' Critical Studies of Ibsen and Björnson, 1899.]

CONTENTS

THE NEWLY-MARRIED COUPLE

A

DRAMATIS PERSONÆ

The FATHER.
The MOTHER.
LAURA, their daughter.
AXEL, her husband.
MATHILDE, her friend.

THE NEWLY-MARRIED COUPLE

ACT I

(SCENE.—*A handsomely furnished, carpeted room, with a
door at the back leading to a lobby. The* FATHER *is
sitting on a couch on the left-hand side, in the foreground,
reading a newspaper. Other papers are lying on a
small table in front of him.* AXEL *is on another couch
drawn up in a similar position on the right-hand side.
A newspaper, which he is not reading, is lying on his
knee. The* MOTHER *is sitting, sewing, in an easy-chair
drawn up beside a table in the middle of the room.*)

LAURA *enters.*

Laura. Good morning, mother! (*Kisses her.*)

Mother. Good morning, dear. Have you slept well?

Laura. Very well, thanks. Good morning, dad! (*Kisses
him.*)

Father. Good morning, little one, good morning. Happy
and in good spirits?

Laura. Very. (*Passes in front of* AXEL.) Good morning, Axel! (*Sits down at the table, opposite her mother.*)

Axel. Good morning.

Mother. I am very sorry to say, my child, that I must
give up going to the ball with you to-night. It is such a
long way to go, in this cold spring weather.

Father (*without looking up from his paper*). Your mother
is not well. She was coughing in the night.

Laura. Coughing again?

3

Father. Twice. (*The* MOTHER *coughs, and he looks up.*) There, do you hear that? Your mother must not go out, on any account.

Laura. Then I won't go, either.

Father. That will be just as well; it is such raw weather. (*To the* MOTHER.) But you have no shawl on, my love; where is your shawl?

Laura. Axel, fetch mother's shawl; it is hanging in the lobby. (AXEL *goes out into the lobby.*)

Mother. We are not really into spring yet. I am surprised the stove is not lit in here.

Laura (*to* AXEL, *who is arranging the shawl over the* MOTHER'S *shoulders*). Axel, ring the bell and let us have a fire. (*He does so, and gives the necessary instructions to the* Servant.)

Mother. If none of us are going to the ball, we ought to send them a note. Perhaps you would see to that, Axel?

Axel. Certainly—but will it do for us to stay away from this ball?

Laura. Surely you heard father say that mother has been coughing in the night.

Axel. Yes, I heard; but the ball is being given by the only friend I have in these parts, in your honour and mine. We are the reason of the whole entertainment— surely we cannot stay away from it?

Laura. But it wouldn't be any pleasure to us to go without mother.

Axel. One often has to do what is not any pleasure.

Laura. When it is a matter of duty, certainly. But our first duty is to mother, and we cannot possibly leave her alone at home when she is ill.

Axel. I had no idea she was ill.

Father (*as he reads*). She coughed twice in the night. She coughed only a moment ago.

Mother. Axel means that a cough or two isn't illness, and he is quite right.

Father (*still reading*). A cough may be a sign of something very serious. (*Clears his throat.*) The chest—or the lungs. (*Clears his throat again.*) I don't think I feel quite the thing myself, either.

Laura. Daddy dear, you are too lightly clothed.

Mother. You dress as if it were summer—and it certainly isn't that.

Father. The fire will burn up directly. (*Clears his throat again.*) No, not quite the thing at all.

Laura. Axel! (*He goes up to her.*) You might read the paper to us till breakfast is ready.

Axel. Certainly. But first of all I want to know if we really are not to go to the ball?

Laura. You can go, if you like, and take our excuses.

Mother. That wouldn't do. Remember you are married now.

Axel. That is exactly why it seems to me that Laura cannot stay at home. The fact that she is my wife ought to have most weight with her now; and this ball is being given for us two, who have nothing the matter with us, besides being mainly a dance for young people—

Mother. And not for old folk.

Laura. Thank you; mother has taken to dancing again since I have grown up. I have never been to a ball without mother's leading off the dances.

Mother. Axel apparently thinks it would have been much better if I had not done so.

Father (*as he reads*). Mother dances most elegantly.

Axel. Surely I should know that, seeing how often I have had the honour of leading off with mother. But on this occasion forty or fifty people have been invited, a lot of trouble and expense incurred and a lot of pleasure arranged, solely for our sakes. It would be simply wicked to disappoint them.

Father (still reading). We can give a ball for them, in return.

Mother. All the more as we owe heaps of people an invitation.

Laura. Yes, that will be better; we have more room here, too. (*A pause.*)

Axel (leaning over LAURA'S *chair*). Think of your new ball dress—my first present to you. Won't that tempt you? Blue muslin, with silver stars all over it? Shall they not shine for the first time to-night?

Laura (smiling). No, there would be no shine in the stars if mother were not at the dance.

Axel. Very well—I will send our excuses. (*Turns to go out.*)

Father (still reading). Perhaps it will be better for me to write. (AXEL *stops.*)

Mother. Yes, you will do it best.

MATHILDE *comes in, followed by a* Servant, *who throws the doors open.*

Mathilde. Breakfast is ready.

Father (taking his wife's arm). Keep your shawl on, my dear; it is cold in the hall. (*They go out.*)

Axel (as he offers LAURA *his arm and leads her towards the door*). Let me have a word with you, before we follow them!

Laura. But it is breakfast time.

Axel (to MATHILDE, *who is standing behind them waiting*). Do you mind going on? (MATHILDE *goes out, followed by the* Servant. AXEL *turns to* LAURA.) Will nothing move you? Go with me to this dance!

Laura. I thought that was what you were going to say.

Axel. For *my* sake!

Laura. But you saw for yourself that mother and father do not wish it?

Axel. I wish it.

Laura. When mother and father do not?

Axel. Then I suppose you are their daughter in the first place, and my wife only in the second?

Laura (with a laugh). Well, that is only natural.

Axel. No, it is not natural; because two days ago you promised to forsake your father and your mother and follow me.

Laura (laughing). To the ball? I certainly never promised that.

Axel. Wherever I wish.

Laura. But you mustn't wish that, Axel darling— because it is quite impossible.

Axel. It is quite possible, if you like to do it.

Laura. Yes, but I don't like.

Axel. That same day you also heard that a man is his wife's lord and master. You must be willing to leave them, if I wish it; it was on those terms that you gave me your hand, you obstinate little woman.

Laura. It was just so as to be able to be always with father and mother, that I did it.

Axel. So that was it. Then you have no wish to be always with *me ?*

Laura. Yes—but not to forsake them.

Axel. Never?

Laura. Never? *(Softly.)* Yes, some day — when I must.

Axel. When must you?

Laura. When? When mother and father—are gone. But why think about such things?

Axel. Don't cry, darling! Listen to me. Would you never be willing to follow me—until they have left us?

Laura. No!—how can you think so?

Axel. Ah, Laura, you don't love me.

Laura. Why do you say such a thing? You only want to make me unhappy.

Axel. You don't even know what love is.

Laura. I don't?—That is not kind of you.

Axel. Tell me what it is then, sweetheart!

Laura (kissing him). Now you mustn't talk about it any more; because you know, if you do, I shall have red eyes, and then father and mother will want to know why they are red, and I shall not be able to tell them, and it will be very embarrassing.

Axel. Better a few tears now than many later on.

Laura. But what have I done to cry about?

Axel. You have given your hand without giving your heart with it; your tongue said " yes," but not your will; you have given yourself without realising what it means. And so, what ought to be the greatest and purest happiness in my life begins to turn to sorrow, and the future looks dark.

Laura. Oh, dear!—and is all this my fault?

Axel. No, it is my own fault. I have been deluding myself with flattering hopes. I thought it would be so easy a matter for my love to awaken yours; but I cannot make you understand me. Every way I have tried has failed. So I must call up my courage, and try the last chance.

Laura. The last chance? What do you mean?

Axel. Laura, I can't tell you how dearly I love you!

Laura. If you did, you wouldn't hurt me. I never hurt you.

Axel. Well, give in to me in just this one thing, and I

shall believe it is the promise of more. Go with me to the ball!

Laura. You know I cannot do that!

Axel. Ah! then I dare not delay any longer!

Laura. You frighten me! You look so angry.

Axel. No, no. But things cannot go on like this any longer. I can't stand it!

Laura. Am I so bad, then? No one ever told me so before.

Axel. Don't cry, my dainty little fairy. You have nothing to blame yourself for—except for being so bewitchingly sweet whether you are laughing or crying. You exhale sweetness like a flower. I want your influence to pervade every place where I am, to distract me when I am moody and laugh away my longings. Hush, hush—no red eyes. Let no one see that. Here is your mother coming—no, it is Mathilde.

Enter MATHILDE.

Mathilde. Your coffee is getting cold.

Axel. We are just coming. At least, Laura is. I want to speak to you for a moment, if I may.

Mathilde. To me?

Axel. If you will allow me.

Mathilde. By all means.

Laura. But you are coming in to breakfast?

Axel. In a moment, darling.

Laura. And you are not angry with me any longer?

Axel (*following her*). I never was that. I never could be!

Laura. I am so glad! (*Runs out.*)

Mathilde. What is it you want?

Axel. Can you keep a secret?

Mathilde. No.

Axel. You won't?

Mathilde. No.

Axel. You won't share any more confidences with me? *(Takes her hand.)* You used to—

Mathilde (drawing back her hand and moving away from him). Yes, I used to.

Axel. Why won't you any longer? *(Goes up to her.)* What is changed?

Mathilde. You. You are married now.

Axel. No, that is just what I am not.

Mathilde. Indeed.

Axel. You have sharp eyes. You must have seen that.

Mathilde. I thought it was all just as you wished.

Axel. You are giving me very abrupt answers. Have I offended you?

Mathilde. What makes you ask that?

Axel. Because lately you have avoided me. Remember how kind you were to me once—indeed, that I owe you everything. It was through you, you know, that I got at her. I had to make assignations with you, in order to meet her. I had to offer you my arm so as to be able to give her the other, and to talk to you so that she might hear my voice. The little darling thought she was doing you a service—

Mathilde. When as a matter of fact it was I that was doing her one—

Axel. Yes, and without suspecting it! That was the amusing part of it.

Mathilde. Yes, that was the amusing part of it.

Axel. But soon people began to say that you and I were secretly engaged, and that we were making a stalking-horse of Laura; so for her sake I had to bring matters to a head rather quickly.

Mathilde. Yes, you took a good many people by surprise.

Axel. Including even yourself, I believe—not to mention the old folk and Laura.   But the worst of it is that I took my own happiness by surprise, too.

Mathilde. What do you mean?

Axel. Of course I knew Laura was only a child; but I thought she would grow up when she felt the approach of love.   But she has never felt its approach; she is like a bud that will not open, and I cannot warm the atmosphere. But you could do that—you, in whom she has confided all her first longings—you, whose kind heart knows so well how to sacrifice its happiness for others.   You know you are to some extent responsible, too, for the fact that the most important event in her life came upon her a little unpreparedly; so you ought to take her by the hand and guide her first steps away from her parents and towards me—direct her affections towards me—

Mathilde. I?   (*A pause.*)

Axel. Won't you?

Mathilde. No—

Axel. But why not?   You love her, don't you?

Mathilde. I do; but this is a thing—

Axel. —that you can do quite well!   For you are better off than the rest of us—you have many more ways of reaching a person's soul than we have.   Sometimes when we have been discussing something, and then you have given your opinion, it has reminded me of the refrains to the old ballads, which sum up the essence of the whole poem in two lines.

Mathilde. Yes, I have heard you flatter before.

Axel. I flatter?   Why, what I have just asked you to do is a clearer proof than anything else how great my—

Mathilde. Stop, stop!   I won't do it!

Axel. Why not? At least be frank with me!

Mathilde. Because—oh, because— (*Turns away.*)

Axel. But what has made you so unkind? (MATHILDE *stops for a moment, as though she were going to answer; then goes hurriedly out.*) What on earth is the matter with her? Has anything gone wrong between her and Laura? Or is it something about the house that is worrying her? She is too level-headed to be disturbed by trifles.—Well, whatever it is, it must look after itself; I have something else to think about. If the one of them *can't* understand me, and the other *won't,* and the old couple neither can nor will, I must act on my own account—and the sooner the better! Later on, it would look to other people like a rupture. It must be done now, before we settle down to this state of things; for if we were to do that, it would be all up with us. To acquiesce in such an unnatural state of affairs would be like crippling one's self on purpose. I am entangled hand and foot here in the meshes of a net of circumspection. I shall have to sail along at " dead slow " all my life—creep about among their furniture and their flowers as warily as among their habits. You might just as well try to stand the house on its head as to alter the slightest thing in it. I daren't move!—and it is becoming unbearable. Would it be a breach of a law of nature to move this couch a little closer to the wall, or this chair further away from it? And has it been ordained from all eternity that this table must stand just where it does? *Can* it be shifted? (*Moves it.*) It actually can! And the couch, too. Why does it stand so far forward? (*Pushes it back.*) And why are these chairs everlastingly in the way? This one shall stand there—and this one there. (*Moves them.*) I will have room for my legs; I positively believe I have forgotten how to walk. For a whole year I have hardly heard the sound of my own footstep—

or-of my own voice; they do nothing but whisper and cough here. I wonder if I have any voice left? (*Sings.*)

> " Bursting every bar and band,
> My fetters will I shatter;
> Striding out, with sword in hand,
> Where the fight "—

(*He stops abruptly, at the entrance of the* FATHER, *the* MOTHER, LAURA *and* MATHILDE, *who have come hurriedly from the breakfast table. A long pause.*)

Laura. Axel, dear!

Mathilde. What, all by himself?

Mother. Do you think you are at a ball?

Father. And playing the part of musician as well as dancer?

Axel. I am amusing myself.

Father. With our furniture?

Axel. I only wanted to see if it was possible to move it.

Mother. If it was possible to move it?

Laura. But what were you shouting about?

Axel. I only wanted to try if I had any voice left.

Laura. If you had any voice left?

Mother. There is a big wood near the house, where you can practise that.

Father. And a waterfall—if you are anxious to emulate Demosthenes.

Laura. Axel, dear—are you out of your mind?

Axel. No, but I think I soon shall be.

Mother. Is there anything wrong?

Axel. Yes, a great deal.

Mother. What is it? Some unpleasant news by post?

Axel. No, not that—but I am unhappy.

Mother. Two days after your wedding?

Father. You have a very odd way of showing it.

Axel. I am taken like that sometimes.

Mother. But what is it? Evidently you are not as happy as we hoped you would be. Confide in us, Axel; we are your parents now, you know.

Axel. It is something I have been thinking about for a long time, but have not had the courage to mention.

Mother. Why? Aren't we good to you?

Axel. You are much too good to me.

Father. What do you mean by that?

Axel. That everything is made far too smooth for me here; my faculties get no exercise; I cannot satisfy my longing for activity and conflict—nor my ambition.

Father. Dear me! What do you want, if you please?

Axel. I want to work for myself, to owe my position in life to my own efforts—to become something.

Father. Really.—What a foolish idea! (*Moves towards the door.*)

Mother. But an idea we must take an interest in. He is our child's husband now, remember. What do you want to be, my boy? Member of Parliament?

Axel. No; but my uncle, who has about the largest legal practice in these parts, offered long ago to hand it over to me.

Mother. But you wouldn't be able to look after it from here, would you, Axel?

Father (*at the door*). A ridiculous idea!—Come back to breakfast. (*Turns to go.*)

Mother. That is true, isn't it? You couldn't look after it from here?

Axel. No; but I can move into town.

All. Move into town? (*A pause. The* FATHER *turns back from the door.*)

Father. That is still more impossible, of course.

Mother. There must be something at the bottom of this. Is anything worrying you? (*Lowering her voice.*) Are you in debt?

Axel. No, thanks to the kindness of you two. You have freed me from that.

Mother. Then what is it, Axel? You have been so strange lately—what is it, my dear boy?

Father. Nonsensical ideas — probably his stomach is disordered. Remember the last time I ate lobster!— Come along in and have a glass of sherry, and you will forget all about it.

Axel. No, it isn't a thing one can forget. It is always in my thoughts—more and more insistently. I must have work for my mind—some outlet for my ambition. I am bored here.

Mother. Two days after your wedding!

Father. Set to work then, for heaven's sake! What is there to hinder you? Would you like to take charge of one of my farms? Or to start some improvements on the estate?—or anything you please! I have no doubt you have ideas, and I will provide the money—only do not let us have any of this fuss!

Axel. But then I shall be indebted to you for everything, and shall feel dependent.

Father. So you would rather feel indebted to your uncle?

Axel. He will give me nothing. I must buy it from him.

Father. Really!—How?

Axel. With my work and my—. Oh well, I suppose you would lend me a little capital?

Father. Not a penny.

Axel. But why?

Father. I will tell you why. Because my son in law

must be my son-in-law, and not a speculating lawyer who sits with his door open and a sign hung out to beg for custom.

Axel. Is a lawyer's profession a dishonourable one, then?

Father. No, it is not. But you have been received into one of the oldest and richest families in the country, and you owe some respect to its traditions. Generation after generation, from time immemorial, the heads of our family have been lords of the manor—not office seekers or fortune hunters. The honourable offices I have held have all been offered to me and not sought by me; and I am not going to have you chattering about your university degree or your talents. You shall stay quietly here, and you will be offered more than you want.

Mother. Come, come, my dear, don't get heated over it; that always makes you so unwell. Let us arrive at some arrangement without wrangling. Axel, you must be reasonable; you know he cannot stand any over-exertion. Laura, get your father a glass of water. Come, my dear, let us go back to the dining-room.

Father. Thanks, I have no appetite left now.

Mother. There, you see!—Axel, Axel!

Laura. For shame, Axel!

Mother. Sit down, dear, sit down! My goodness, how hot you are!

Father. It is so warm in here.

Mother. That is the stove. Shut it down, Mathilde!

Laura (to AXEL). You are a nice one, I must say!

Father. The chairs—put them straight! (*They do so.*) And the table! (*They do so.*) That is better.

Mother. That is the worst of a stranger in the house—something of this sort may so easily happen.

Father. But a thing like this!—I have never in my life been contradicted before.

Mother. It is for the first and last time! He will soon learn who you are and what is due to you.

Father. And to think that, the first time, it should be my son-in-law that—

Mother. He will regret it for the rest of your life, you may be sure, and when you are gone he will have no peace of mind. We can only hope that the atmosphere of affection in this house will improve him. Really, lately, Axel has behaved as if he were bewitched.

Laura. Yes, hasn't he?

Mother. Good gracious, Laura, do you mean that you—

Laura. No, I didn't mean anything.

Mother. Laura, are you trying to conceal something?

Father. And from us? (*Gets up.*) Are things as bad as that?

Laura. I assure you, dear people, it is nothing; it is only—

Father and Mother (*together*). Only—?

Laura. No, no, it is nothing—only you frighten me so.

Father and Mother (*together*). She is crying!

Mathilde. She is crying!

Father. Now, sir—why is she crying?

Laura. But, father, father—look, I am not crying the least bit.

Mother and Mathilde. Yes, she is crying!

Axel. Yes—and will cry every day until we make a change here! (*A pause, while they all look at him.*) Well, as so much has been said, it may as well all come out. Our marriage is not a happy one, because it lacks the most essential thing of all.

Mother. Merciful heavens, what are you saying!

Father. Compose yourself; let me talk to him. What do you mean, sir?

Axel. Laura does not love me—

B

Laura. Yes, that is what he says!

Axel. She hasn't the least idea what love means, and will never learn as long as she is in her father's house.

Mother and Father. Why?

Axel. Because she lives only for her parents; me, she looks upon merely as an elder brother who is to assist her in loving them.

Mother. Is that so distasteful to you, then?

Axel. No, no. I am devoted to you and grateful to you, and I am proud of being your son; but it is only through her that I am that—and she has never yet really taken me to her heart. I am quite at liberty to go away or to stay, as I please; *she* is a fixture here. There is never one of her requests to me, scarcely a single wish she expresses—indeed, scarcely a sign of endearment she shows me, that she has not first of all divided up into three portions; and I get my one-third of it, and get it last or not at all.

Mother. He is jealous—and of us!

Father. Jealous of us!

Laura. Yes, indeed he is, mother.

Father. This is mere fancy, Axel—a ridiculous idea. Do not let any one else hear you saying that.

Axel. No, it is neither mere fancy nor is it ridiculous. It colours the whole of our relations to one another; it gnaws at my feelings, and then I torment her, make you angry, and lead an idle, empty, ill-tempered existence—

Father. You are ill, there is no doubt about it.

Axel. I am, and you have made me ill.

Father and Mother (*together*). We have?

Father. Please be a little—

Axel. You allow her to treat me simply as the largest sized of all the dolls you have given her to play with.

You cannot bear to see her give away any more of her affection than she might give to one of her dolls.

Father. Please talk in a more seemly manner! Please show us a proper respect—

Axel. Forgive me, my dear parents, if I don't. What I mean is that a child cannot be a wife, and as long as she remains with you she will always be a child.

Mother. But, Axel, did we not tell you she was only a child—

Father. We warned you, we asked you to wait a year or two—

Mother. Because we could not see that she loved you sufficiently.

Father. But your answer was that it was just the child in her that you loved.

Mother. Just the child's innocence and simplicity. You said you felt purer in her presence; indeed, that she sometimes made you feel as if you were in church. And we, her father and mother, understood that, for we had felt it ourselves.

Father. We felt that just as much as you, my son.

Mother. Do you remember one morning, when she was asleep, that you said her life was a dream which it would be a sin to disturb?

Father. And said that the mere thought of her made you tread more softly for fear of waking her.

Axel. That is quite true. Her childlike nature shed happiness upon me, her gentle innocence stilled me. It is quite true that I felt her influence upon my senses like that of a beautiful morning.

Father. And now you are impatient with her for being a child!

Axel. Exactly! At the time when I was longing to lead her to the altar, I daresay I only thought of her as an inspiration to my better self and my best impulses. She was to me what the Madonna is to a good Catholic; but now she has become something more than that. The distance between us no longer exists; I cannot be satisfied with mere adoration, I must love; I cannot be satisfied with kneeling to her, I need my arms around her. Her glance has the same delicacy it always had, the same innocence; but I can no longer sit and gaze at her by the hour. Her glance must lose itself in mine in complete surrender. Her hand, her arm, her mouth are the same as they were; but I need to feel her hand stroking my hair, her arm round my neck, her mouth on mine; her thoughts must embrace mine and be like sunshine in my heart. She was a symbol to me, but the symbol has become flesh and blood. When first she came into my thoughts it was as a child; but I have watched her day by day grow into a woman, whose shyness and ignorance make her turn away from me, but whom I must possess. (LAURA *moves quickly towards him.*)

Mother. He loves our child!

Father. He loves her! (*Embraces his wife.*) What more is there to say, then? Everything is as it should be. Come along and have a glass of sherry!

Axel. No, everything is not as it should be. I can get her gratitude sometimes in a lucky moment, but not her heart. If I am fond of a certain thing, she is not. If I wish a thing, she wishes the opposite—for instance, if it's only a question of going to a ball, she won't take any pleasure in it unless her mother can go too.

Mother. Good heavens, is it nothing but that!

Laura. No, mother, it is nothing else; it is this ball.

Father. Then for any sake go to the ball! You are a couple of noodles. Come along, now.

Axel. The ball? It is not the ball. I don't care a bit about the ball.

Laura. No, that is just it, mother. When he gets what he wants, it turns out that it wasn't what he wanted at all, but something quite different. I don't understand what it is.

Axel. No, because it is not a question of any one thing, but of our whole relations to one another. Love is what I miss; she does not know what it means, and never will know—as long as she remains at home here. (*A pause.*)

Mother (*slowly*). As long as she remains at home?

Father (*coming nearer to him, and trembling slightly*). What do you mean by that?

Axel. It will be only when Laura finds she can no longer lean upon her parents, that she may possibly come to lean upon me.

Mother. What does he mean?

Father. I don't understand—

Axel. If she is to be something more than a good daughter—if she is to be a good wife—Laura must go away from here.

Mother. Laura go away?

Father. Our child?

Laura (*to her* MOTHER). Mother!

Axel. It would be wronging her whom I love so deeply, it would be wronging myself, and wronging you who mean so well, if now, when the power is in my hands, I had not the spirit to make use of it. Here, Laura lives only for you; when you die, life will be over for her. But that is not what marriage means, that is not what she promised at the altar, and that is what I cannot submit to. To go on like this will only make us all unhappy; and that is why Laura must go with me! (*The* MOTHER *starts forward ;* LAURA *goes to* MATHILDE.)

Father. You cannot mean what you say.

Axel. I am in deadly earnest, and no one can shake my resolution.

Mother. Then Heaven have mercy on us! (*A pause.*)

Father. You know, Axel, that God gave us five children; and you know, too, that He took four away from us again. Laura is now our only child, our only joy.

Mother. We can't bear to lose her, Axel! She has never been away from us a single day since she was born. She is the spoilt child of our sorrow; if death itself claimed her, we should have to hold fast on to her.

Father. Axel, you are not a wicked man; you have not come amongst us to make us all unhappy?

Axel. If I were to give in now, this state of things would occur again every week or so, and none of us could stand that. For that reason, my dear parents, prove yourselves capable of a sacrifice. Let us put an end to it once for all—and let Laura move into town with me next week.

Father. Good heavens—it is impossible!

Mother. You won't have the heart to do that. Look at her, and then say that again! (AXEL *turns away.*) No, I knew you could not. (*To the* FATHER.) You talk to him! Tell him the truth, set him right, since he has broken in upon a good and loving family only to bring misfortune to it.

Father. In this house, as far back as I can remember, no hard words have ever been used. It seems to me like some evil dream, that I am struggling to wake out of and cannot! (*A pause.*) Mr. Hargaut, when we gave our daughter to you, we made no conditions. We admitted you into a happy family, to a position of wealth, to a promising future; and we expected, in return, some little affection, some little appreciation—at least some little respect. But you behave like—like a stranger, who is admitted to one's intimacy and good offices, and then one morning goes off with the most valuable possessions in the house — like an ungrateful, cruel—! We have confided our child, the dearest, sweetest child, our only child, to—a man without a heart! We were two happy parents, rich in her love—parents whom every one envied —and we now are two poor bereaved wretches, who must creep away together into a corner in their unhappy disillusionment. (*Sits down.*)

Mother. And this is the way you can treat the man who has given you everything! What answer have you to give him?

Axel. It makes my heart bleed. If I had thought it would be as hard as this, indeed I would never have begun it; but if we leave the matter unsettled, now that it has been broached, we shall never be on proper terms with one another again. Of that I am certain. If it is a matter that pains us all, for that very reason let us go through with it and get it settled.

Father. Poor confiding fools that we have been!

Mother. Can't you give us some respite, so that we may think things over quietly? This is simply tearing us apart.

Axel. It would only prolong your pain, and it would end in your hating me. No, it must be done now—at once; otherwise it will never be done.

Mother. Oh dear, oh dear! (*Sits down.*)

Father. Axel! Listen to us for a moment! It is quite possible you may be in the right; but for that very reason I beg you—I, who have never yet begged anything of any one—I beg you, be merciful! I am an old man, and cannot stand it—and she (*looking at his wife*) still less.

Axel. Ah, I am not hard-hearted—but I must try to be

resolute.   If I lose now, I shall be losing her for life, I know.   Therefore she *shall* go with me!

Mother (*springing up*).   No, she shall not!   If you loved her, as you say you do, you hypocrite, you would remain where she is—and here she shall stay!

Laura (*who has been standing beside* MATHILDE, *goes to her* MOTHER).   Yes, to my dying day.

Father (*getting up*).   No!   We must not alter God's law.   It is written: "A man shall forsake his father and his mother, and cleave only unto his wife"—and in the same way she must cleave only to him.   Laura shall go when he wishes.

Laura.   Father, can you—have you the heart to—?

Father.   No, I haven't the heart to, my child.   But I shall do it nevertheless, because it is right.   Oh, Laura!— (*Embraces her.   The* MOTHER *joins her embrace to his*.)

Mathilde (*to* AXEL).   You Jesuit!—You have no consideration, no mercy; you trample upon hearts as you would upon the grass that grows in your path.   But you shall not find this so easy as you think.   It is true she is a child—but I shall go with her!   I don't know you, and I don't trust you.   (*Clenches her fist*.)   But I shall watch over her!

Curtain.

ACT II

(SCENE.—AXEL'S *house, a year later. The room is arranged almost identically like that in the first act. Two large portraits of* LAURA'S *parents, very well executed, hang in full view.* LAURA *is sitting at the table,* MATHILDE *on the couch on the right.*)

Mathilde (*reading aloud from a book*). "'No,' was the decided answer. Originally it was he that was to blame, but now it is she. He tore her from her parents, her home and her familiar surroundings; but since then he has sought her forgiveness so perseveringly, and her love so humbly, that it would take all the obstinacy of a spoilt child to withstand him. Just as formerly he could think of nothing but his love, so now she will consider nothing except her self-love; but she is so much the more to blame than he, as her motives are less good than his. She is like a child that has woke up too early in the morning; it strikes and kicks at any one that comes to pet it."

Laura. Mathilde—does it really say that?

Mathilde. Indeed it does.

Laura. Just as you read it?

Mathilde. Look for yourself.

Laura (*takes the book and looks at it, then lays it down*). It is almost our own story, word for word. I would give anything to know who has written it.

Mathilde. It is a mere coincidence—

Laura. No, some wicked wretch has seen something like this—some creature that is heartless enough to be able to mock at a parent's love; it must be some one

25

who either is worthless himself or has had worthless parents!

Mathilde. Why, Laura, how seriously you take it!

Laura. Yes, it irritates me, this libelling of all fidelity. What is fidelity, if it does not mean that a child should be true to its parents?

Mathilde. But I was just reading to you about that. (*Reads.*) " The object of fidelity changes, as we ourselves change. The child's duty is to be true to its parents; the married, to one another; the aged, to their children—"

Laura. Don't read any more! I won't hear any more! Its whole train of thought offends me. (*After a pause.*) What a horrid book! (*Indifferently.*) What happens to them in the end?

Mathilde (*in the same tone*). To whom?

Laura. That couple—in the book.

Mathilde (*still in an indifferent tone*). It doesn't end happily. (*A pause.*)

Laura (*looking up*). Which of them suffers?

Mathilde. Which do you think?

Laura (*beginning to sew again*). She, I should think— because she is unhappy already.

Mathilde. You have guessed right. She falls in love.

Laura (*astonished*). Falls in love?

Mathilde. Yes. Some time or other, love is awakened in the heart of every woman; and then, if she cannot love her husband, in the course of time she will love some one else.

Laura (*dismayed*). Some one else!

Mathilde. Yes. (*A pause.*)

Laura. That is horrible! (*Begins to sew, then lays her hand down on the table, then begins to sew again.*) And what happens to him?

Mathilde. He falls ill, very ill. And then some one finds him out and comforts him—a woman.

Laura (*looking up*). How does that happen?

Mathilde. His heart is like an empty house, in an atmosphere of sadness and longing.   Little by little she— the woman who comforts him—creeps into it; and so in time there comes the day when he can say he is happy. (*A pause.*)

Laura (*quietly*). Who is she?

Mathilde. One of those poor-spirited creatures that can be content with the aftermath of love.

Laura (*after a pause, during which she has been looking fixedly at* MATHILDE). Could you be that?

Mathilde. No!—I must be first or nothing!

Laura. But about her?

Mathilde. The wife?

Laura. Yes.   What happens to her?

Mathilde. Directly she realises that love for another has taken possession of her husband, she turns towards him with all her heart; but it is too late then.   (LAURA *sits absorbed for a few moments ; then gets up hurriedly and goes to a little work-table that is standing at the end of the couch on the left, opens it, looks for something in it, stops to think, then looks in it again.*)   What are you looking for?

Laura. A photograph.

Mathilde. Axel's?

Laura. No—but what has become of it?

Mathilde. Don't you remember that one day you took it up and said you would not have it?   So I hid it.

Laura. You?

Mathilde. Yes—till you should ask about it.   (*Gets up, opens her work-table that stands by the right-hand couch.*) Here it is.   (*Gives it to her.*)

Laura. So you have got it!   (*Lays it in her table drawer without looking at it, shuts the drawer, goes a few paces away,*

then comes back, turns the key in the drawer and takes it out.)
Has Axel read the new book?

Mathilde. I don't know. Shall I give it to him?

Laura. Just as you like. Perhaps you would like to
read it aloud to him. (*A* Maid *comes in with a letter;*
LAURA *takes it, and the* Maid *goes out again.*) From my
parents! (*Kisses the letter with emotion.*) The only ones
who love me! (*Goes out hurriedly. At the same moment*
AXEL *comes in from the outer door.*)

Axel. She always goes when I come in!

Mathilde (*getting up*). This time it was an accident,
though. (*Looks at him.*) How pale you are!

Axel (*seriously*). I am rather worried.—Have you read
the new novel?

Mathilde (*putting the book in her pocket*). What
novel?

Axel. " The Newly-Married Couple "—quite a small
book.

Mathilde. Oh, that one—I have just been reading it.

Axel (*eagerly*). And Laura too? Has Laura read it?

Mathilde. She thinks it is a poor story.

Axel. It isn't that, but it is an extraordinary one. It
quite startles me—it is like coming into one's own room
and seeing one's self sitting there. It has caught hold of
unformed thoughts that lie hidden deep in my soul.

Mathilde. Every good book does that.

Axel. Everything will happen to me just as it does
in that book; the premises are all here, only I had not
recognised them.

Mathilde. I have heard of very young doctors feeling
the symptoms of all the diseases they read about.

Axel. Oh, but this is more than mere imagination.
My temptations come bodily before me. My thoughts
are the result of what happens, just as naturally as smoke

is the result of fire — and these thoughts (*glancing at* MATHILDE) lead me far.

Mathilde. As far as I can see, the book only teaches consideration for a woman, especially if she is young.

Axel. That is true. But, look here—a young man, brought up among students, cannot possibly possess, ready-made, all this consideration that a woman's nature requires. He doesn't become a married man in one day, but by degrees. He cannot make a clean sweep of his habits and take up the silken bonds of duty, all in a moment. The inspiration of a first love gives him the capacity, but he has to learn how to use it. I never saw what I had neglected till I had frightened her away from me. But what is there that I have not done, since then, to win her? I have gone very gently to work and tried from every side to get at her—I have tempted her with gifts and with penitence—but you can see for yourself she shrinks from me more and more. My thoughts, wearied with longings and with the strain of inventing new devices, follow her, and my love for her only grows—but there are times when such thoughts are succeeded by a void so great that my whole life seems slipping away into it. It is then I need some one to cling to—. Oh, Mathilde, you have meant very much to me at times like that. (*Goes up to her.*)

Mathilde (*getting up*). Yes, all sorts of things happen in a year that one never thought of at the beginning of it.

Axel (*sitting down*). Good God, what a year! I haven't the courage to face another like it. This book has frightened me.

Mathilde (*aside*). That's a good thing, anyway.

Axel (*getting up*). Besides—the amount of work I have to do, to keep up everything here just as she was accustomed to have it, is getting to be too much for me, Mathilde. It won't answer in the long run. If only I had the reward of thanks that the humblest working-man gets—if it were only a smile; but when I have been travelling about for a week at a time, exposed to all sorts of weather in these open boats in winter, do I get any welcome on my home-coming? When I sit up late, night after night, does she ever realise whom I am doing it for? Has she as much as noticed that I have done so—or that I have, at great expense, furnished this house like her parents'? No, she takes everything as a matter of course; and if any one were to say to her, "He has done all this for your sake," she would merely answer, "He need not have done so, I had it all in my own home."

Mathilde. Yes, you have come to a turning-point now.

Axel. What do you mean?

Mathilde. Nothing particular—here she comes!

Axel. Has anything happened? She is in such a hurry!

LAURA *comes in with an open letter in her hand.*

Laura (in a low voice, to MATHILDE). Mother and father are so lonely at home that they are going abroad, to Italy; but they are coming here, Mathilde, before they leave the country.

Mathilde. Coming here? When?

Laura. Directly. I hadn't noticed—the letter is written from the nearest posting station; they want to take us by surprise—they will be here in a few minutes. Good heavens, what are we to do?

Mathilde (quickly). Tell Axel that!

Laura. I tell him?

Mathilde. Yes, you must.

Laura (in a frightened voice). I?

Mathilde (to AXEL). Laura has something she wants to tell you.

Laura. Mathilde!

Axel. This is something new.

Laura. Oh, do tell him, Mathilde. (MATHILDE *says nothing, but goes to the back of the room.*)

Axel (*coming up to her*). What is it?

Laura (*timidly*). My parents are coming.

Axel. Here?

Laura. Yes.

Axel. When? To-day?

Laura. Yes. Almost directly.

Axel. And no one has told me! (*Takes up his hat to go.*)

Laura (*frightened*). Axel!

Axel. It is certainly not for the pleasure of finding me here that they are coming.

Laura. But you mustn't go!

Mathilde. No, you mustn't do that.

Axel. Are they not going to put up here?

Laura. Yes, I thought—if you are willing—in your room.

Axel. So that is what it is to be—I am to go away and they are to take my place.

Mathilde. Take my room, and I will move into Laura's. I will easily arrange that. (*Goes out.*)

Axel. Why all this beating about the bush? It is quite natural that you should want to see them, and equally natural that I should remove myself when they come; only you should have broken it to me—a little more considerately. Because I suppose they are coming now to take you with them—and, even if it means nothing to you to put an end to everything like this, at all events you ought to know what it means to me!

Laura. I did not know till this moment that they were coming.

Axel. But it must be your letters that have brought them here—your complaints—

Laura. I have made no complaints.

Axel. You have only told them how matters stand here.

Laura. Never. (*A pause.*)

Axel (*in astonishment*). What have you been writing to them all this year, then—a letter every day?

Laura. I have told them everything was going well here.

Axel. Is it possible? All this time? Laura! Dare I believe it? Such consideration— (*Comes nearer to her.*) Ah, at last, then—?

Laura (*frightened*). I did it out of consideration for them.

Axel (*coldly*). For them? Well, I am sorry for them, then. They will soon see how things stand between us.

Laura. They are only to be here a day or two. Then they go abroad.

Axel. Abroad? But I suppose some one is going with them?—you, perhaps?

Laura. You can't, can you?

Axel. No.—So you are going away from me, Laura!—I am to remain here with Mathilde—it is just like that book.

Laura. With Mathilde? Well—perhaps Mathilde could go with them?

Axel. You know we can't do without her here—as things are at present.

Laura. Perhaps you would rather I—?

Axel. There is no need for you to ask my leave. You go if you wish.

Laura. Yes, you can do without *me.*—All the same, I think I shall stay!

Axel. You will stay—with me?

Laura. Yes.

Axel (in a happier voice, coming up to her). That is not out of consideration for your parents?

Laura. No, that it isn't! (*He draws back in astonishment.* MATHILDE *comes in.*)

Mathilde. It is all arranged. (*To* AXEL.) You will stay, then?

Axel (looking at LAURA). I don't know.—If I go away for these few days, perhaps it will be better.

Mathilde (coming forward). Very well, then I shall go away too!

Laura. You?

Axel. You?

Mathilde. Yes, I don't want to have anything to do with what happens. (*A pause.*)

Axel. What do you think will happen?

Mathilde. That is best left unsaid—till anything does happen. (*A pause.*)

Axel. You are thinking too hardly of your friend now.

Laura (quietly). Mathilde is not my friend.

Axel. Mathilde not your—

Laura (as before). A person who is always deceiving one is no friend.

Axel. Has Mathilde deceived anybody? You are unjust.

Laura (as before). Am I? It is Mathilde's fault that I am unhappy now.

Axel. Laura!

Laura. My dear, you may defend her, if you choose; but you must allow me to tell you plainly that it is Mathilde's advice that has guided me from the days of my innocent childhood, and has led me into all the misery I am suffering now! If it were not for her I should not be married to-day and separated from my parents. She

C

came here with me—not to help me, as she pretended—
but to be able still to spy on me, quietly and secretly, in
her usual way, and afterwards to make use of what she
had discovered.   But she devotes herself to you; because
she — no, I won't say it! (*With growing vehemence.*)
Well, just you conspire against me, you two—and see
whether I am a child any longer!   The tree that you have
torn up by the roots and transplanted will yield you no
fruit for the first year, however much you shake its
branches!   I don't care if things do happen as they do
in that story she has taken such pleasure in reading to
me; but I shall never live to see the day when I shall beg
for any one's love!   And now my parents are coming to
see everything, everything—and that is just what I want
them to do!   Because I won't be led like a child, and I
won't be deceived!   I won't! (*Stands quite still for a
moment, then bursts into a violent fit of crying and runs
out.*)

Axel (*after a pause*). What is the meaning of that?

Mathilde. She hates me.

Axel (*astonished*). When did it come to that?

Mathilde. Little by little.   Is it the first time you have
noticed it?

Axel (*still more astonished*). Have you no longer her
confidence, then?

Mathilde. No more than you.

Axel. She, who once believed every one—!

Mathilde. Now she believes no one. (*A pause.*)

Axel. And what is still more amazing—only there is no
mistaking it—is that she is jealous!

Mathilde. Yes.

Axel. And of you?—When there is not the slightest
foundation—. (*Stops involuntarily and looks at her; she
crosses the room.*)

Mathilde. You should only be glad that this has happened.

Axel. That she is jealous?—or what do you mean?

Mathilde. It has helped her. She is on the high road to loving you now.

Axel. Now?

Mathilde. Love often comes in that way—especially to the one who has been made uneasy.

Axel. And you are to be the scapegoat?

Mathilde. I am accustomed to that.

Axel (*quickly, as he comes nearer to her*). You must have known love yourself, Mathilde?

Mathilde (*starts, then says*). Yes, I have loved too.

Axel. Unhappily?

Mathilde. Not happily. But why do you ask?

Axel. Those who have been through such an experience are less selfish than the rest of us and are capable of more.

Mathilde. Yes. Love is always a consecration, but not always for the same kind of service.

Axel. Sometimes it only brings unhappiness.

Mathilde. Yes, when people have nothing in them, and no pride.

Axel. The more I get to know of you, the less I seem really to know you. What sort of a man can this fellow be, that you have loved without return?

Mathilde (*in a subdued voice*). A man to whom I am now very grateful; because marriage is not my vocation.

Axel. What is your vocation, then?

Mathilde. One that one is unwilling to speak about, until one knows that it has been successful.—And I don't believe I should have discovered it, but for him.

Axel. And is your mind quite at peace now? Have you no longings?

Mathilde (speaking here, and in what follows, with some vehemence). Yes, a longing to travel—a long, long way! To fill my soul with splendid pictures!—Oh, if you have any regard for me—

Axel. I have more than that, Mathilde—the warmest gratitude—and more than that, I—

Mathilde (interrupting him). Well, then, make it up with Laura! Then I shall be able to go abroad with her parents. Oh, if I don't get away—far away—there is something within me that will die!

Axel. Go away then, Mathilde—you say so, and therefore I believe you. ,

Mathilde. But I am not going till you two are reconciled! I don't want all three of us to be unhappy. No, I am not unhappy; but I shall be if you are—and if I don't get abroad now!

Axel. What can I do in the matter?

Mathilde (quickly). Stay here and give the old folk a welcome! Behave to Laura as if there were nothing the matter, and she will say nothing!

Axel. Why do you think she will say nothing?

Mathilde. Because of all I have done to make that likely!

Axel. You?

Mathilde. Yes—no—yes; at least, not as you wanted me to, but indirectly—

Axel. Even at the beginning of all this?

Mathilde. No, not then, it is true. But forget that, because now I have made it good! I did not know you then—and there were reasons—

Axel (going nearer to her). Mathilde, you have filled me with an extraordinary regard for you—as if everything that I have been denied in another quarter was to be found in you, and as if now for the first time I—

Mathilde. There is the carriage!

Axel. What shall I do?

Mathilde. Go down and welcome the old folk! Be quick! Look, Laura is down there already—oh, don't let her miss you just at this moment! There, that is right. (*He goes.*) Yes, that was right; this is my first real victory! (*Goes out. Voices are heard without, and soon afterwards the* MOTHER *comes in with* LAURA, *and after her the* FATHER *with* AXEL *and* MATHILDE.)

Mother. So here I am in your home, my darling child! (*Kisses her.*) It is really worth being separated, for the pleasure of meeting again! (*Kisses her.*) And such nice letters from you, every single day—thank you, darling! (*Kisses her again.*) And you look just the same—just the same! Perhaps a trifle paler, but that is natural. (*Kisses her.*)

Axel (*to the* FATHER, *who is taking off a coat and several comforters*). May I?

Father (*bowing*). Thank you, I can manage quite well myself.

Axel. But let me hang them up for you?

Father. Much obliged—I will do it myself! (*Takes them out into the hall.*)

Mother (*to* LAURA, *in a low voice*). It was hard work to get your father to come, I can tell you. He still cannot forget—. But we had to see our little girl before we set off on our travels; and we had to travel, because it was getting so lonely at home.

Laura. Dear mother! (*She and* MATHILDE *help her to take her things off.*)

Axel (*to the* FATHER, *who has come in again*). I hope you had a pleasant journey, sir?

Father. Remarkably pleasant.

Axel. Caught no cold, I hope?

Father. Nothing to speak of—just a trifle—a slightly

relaxed throat; out late—and heavy dews. You are well?

Axel. Very well, thank you.

Father. I am extremely pleased to hear it.

Mother (to the FATHER). But, do you see—?

Father. What, my love?

Mother. Do you mean to say you don't see?

Father. No, what is it?

Mother. We are at home again! This is our own room over again!

Father (in astonishment). Upon my word—!

Mother. The carpet, the curtains, the furniture, everything—even down to their arrangement in the room! (*Goes across to* AXEL *and takes his hand.*) A more touching proof of your love for her we could never have had! (*To the* FATHER.) Isn't that so?

Father (struggling with his astonishment). Yes, I must say—

Mother. And you never wrote us a single word about this, Laura?

Mathilde. It is not only this room, but the whole house is arranged like yours as far as possible.

Mother. The whole house! Is it possible!

Father. It is the most charming way of giving pleasure to a young wife that I ever heard of!

Mother. I am so astonished, Laura, at your never having mentioned a word of all this in your letters.

Father. Never a word of it!

Mother. Hadn't you noticed it?

Father. Ah, well—what one sees every day, one is apt to think every one knows all about—isn't that it, little girl? That is the explanation, isn't it?

Mother. And Axel has given you all this by his own exertions! Aren't you proud of that?

Father (clapping her on the back). Of course she is, but it was never Laura's way to say much about her feelings; although this is really something so—

Mother (laughing). Her letters lately have been nothing but dissertations upon love.

Laura. Mother!—

Mother. Oh, I am going to tell! But you have a good husband, Laura.

Laura. Mother!—

Mother (in a lower voice). You have paid him some little attentions in return, of course?—given him something, or—

Father (pushing in between them). Worked something for him, eh?

(MATHILDE, *in the meantime, has brought in wine and filled some glasses.*)

Axel. Now, a glass of wine to welcome you—sherry, your favourite wine, sir.

Mother. He remembers that! (*They each take a glass in their hands.*)

Axel. Laura and I bid you heartily welcome here in our house! And we hope you will find everything here—(*with emotion*) just as you would wish it. I will do my best that you shall, and I am sure Laura will too.

Mother. Of course she will!—Drink his health! (AXEL *touches her glass with his; her hand trembles, and she spills some wine.*) You have filled the glasses too full, my dear! (*They all clink glasses and drink.*)

Father (when the glasses have been filled again). My wife and I—thank you very much for your welcome. We could not set out on our journey without first seeing our child—our two children. A good friend of ours (*looking at* MATHILDE) advised us to come unexpectedly. At first we did not want to but now we are glad we did; because now we can see for ourselves that Laura told the truth in her letters. You are happy—and therefore we old folk must be happy too, and bury all recollection of what— what evidently happened for the best. Hm, hm!—At one time we could not think it was so—and that was why we did not wish to be parted from our child; but now we can make our minds quite easy about it—because now we can trust you. I have complete trust in you, Axel, my dear son—God bless you! (*They grasp hands, and drink to each other again.*)

Mother. Do you know what I should like?

All. No!

Mother. I should like Axel to tell us how your reconciliation came about.

Laura. Mother!

Mother. Why should you be shy about it? Why have you never told us about it? Good gracious, didn't you think your parents would be only too glad to hear how lucky their little girl was?

Father. I think it is a very good idea of your mother's. Now let us sit down and hear all about it. (*They sit down ;* LAURA *turns away.*) No, come and sit down beside your mother, Laura! We are going to have a good look at you while he tells us about it. (*Pulls her to him.*)

Mother. And don't forget anything, Axel! Tell us of the very first sign of love, the first little kindness, Laura showed you.

Axel. Yes, I will tell you how it came about.

Laura (*getting up*). But, Axel—!

Axel. I shall only be supplementing what you told in your letters, Laura.

Mother. It is all to your credit, my child! Now be quiet and listen to him, and correct him if he forgets anything. (*Pulls her down to her seat again.*)

Axel. Yes, my dear parents. You know, of course, that we did not begin very well—

Father. Quite so—but you can pass over that.

Axel. As soon as she was left to depend on herself alone, I realised the great wrong I had done to Laura. She used to tremble when I came near her, and before long she used to tremble just as much before any one. At first I felt the humility of a strong man who has triumphed; but after a time I became anxious, for I had acted too strongly. Then I dedicated my love to the task of winning back, in a Jacob's seven years of service, what I had lost in one moment. You see this house—I made everything smooth in it for her feet. You see what we have round us—I set that before her eyes. By means of nights of work, by exerting myself to the uttermost, I got it all together, bit by bit—in order that she should never feel anything strange or inhospitable in her home, but only what she was accustomed to and fond of. She understood; and soon the birds of spring began to flutter about our home. And, though she always ran away when I came, I was conscious of her presence in a hundred little loving touches in my room—at my desk—

Laura (ashamed). Oh, it isn't true!

Axel. Don't believe her! Laura is so kind-hearted—her fear of me made her shy, but she could not withstand her own kind impulses and my humble faithfulness. When I was sitting late in my room, working for her, she was sitting up in hers — at any rate I often thought I heard her footstep; and when I came home late after a wearisome journey, if she did not run to welcome me, it was not because she was wanting in wifely gratitude—Laura has no lack of that—but because she did not wish to betray her happiness till the great day of our reconciliation should come. (LAURA *gets up*.)

Father. Then you were not reconciled immediately?

Axel. Not immediately.

Mother (*anxiously, in a subdued voice*). My goodness, Laura did not say a word about that!

Axel. Because she loved you, and did not want to distress you unnecessarily. But does not her very silence about it show that she was waiting for me? That was her love's first gift to me. (LAURA *sits down again.*) After a while she gave me others. She saw that I was not angry; on the contrary, she saw that where I had erred, I had erred through my love for her; and she is so loving herself, that little by little she schooled herself to meet me in gentle silence—she longed to be a good wife. And then, one lovely morning—just like to-day—we both had been reading a book which was like a voice from afar, threatening our happiness, and we were driven together by fear. Then, all at once, all the doors and windows flew wide open! It was your letter! The room seemed to glow with warmth—just as it does now with you sitting there; summer went singing through the house—and then I saw in her eyes that all the blossoms were going to unfold their petals! Then I knelt down before her, as I do now, and said: For your parents' sake, that they may be happy about us—for my sake, that I may not be punished any longer—for your own sake, that you may be able again to live as the fulness of your kind heart prompts—let us find one another now! And then Laura answered— (LAURA *throws herself into his arms, in a burst of tears. All get up.*)

Mother. That was beautiful, children!

Father. As beautiful as if we were young again ourselves, and had found one another!—How well he told it, too!

Mother. Yes, it was just as if it was all happening before our eyes!

Father. Wasn't it?—He's a very gifted man.

Mother (*in a low voice*). He will do something big!

Father (*in the same tones*). Ay, a big man—and one of our family!

Axel (*who has advanced towards the foreground with* LAURA). So that was your answer, Laura?

Laura. You haven't remembered everything.

Mother. Is there something more? Let us hear some more!

Axel. What did you say, then?

Laura. You know I said that something had held me back a long, long time! I saw well enough that you were fond of me, but I was afraid it was only as you would be fond of a child.

Axel. Laura!

Laura. I am not so clever as—as some others, you know; but I am not a child any longer, because now I love you!

Axel. You *are* a child, all the same!

Father (*to the* MOTHER). But what about our arrangements? We were to have gone on our travels at once.

Axel. No, stay with us a few days now! (LAURA *makes a sign to him.*) Not?

Laura (*softly*). I would rather be alone with you, now.

Mother. What are you saying, Laura?

Laura. I?—I was saying that I should like to ask you, if you are going abroad now, to take Mathilde with you.

Mother. That is very nice of you, Laura, to remember Mathilde. People generally say that newly-married couples think of no one but themselves.

Father. No, Laura is not like that!

All. No, Laura is not like that!

Laura (gently). Mathilde, forgive me! (*They embrace, and* LAURA *says softly:*) I understand you now for the first time!

Mathilde. Not quite.

Laura. I know that I should never have got Axel, but for you.

Mathilde. That is true.

Laura. Oh, Mathilde, I am so happy now!

Mathilde. And I wish you every happiness.

Axel (taking LAURA'S *arm).* Now you may go and travel abroad, Mathilde!

Mathilde. Yes!—and my next book shall be a better one.

Axel. Your next—?

Curtain.

LEONARDA

A PLAY IN FOUR ACTS

DRAMATIS PERSONÆ

The BISHOP.
CORNELIA, his sister.
HAGBART, his nephew.
The GRANDMOTHER.
LEONARDA FALK.
AAGOT, her niece.
GENERAL ROSEN.
CHIEF JUSTICE RÖST.
MRS. RÖST.
PEDERSEN, agent to Mrs. Falk.
HANS.
A Maid.

LEONARDA

ACT I

(Scene.—*A large room in* Leonarda Falk's *house. At the back, folding doors which are standing open. Antique furniture.* Leonarda, *dressed in a riding-habit, is standing beside a writing-desk on the left, talking to her agent* Pedersen.)

Leonarda. It is a complete loss.

Pedersen. But, Mrs. Falk—

Leonarda. A loss, every scrap of it. I can't sell burnt bricks. How much is there of it? Two kilns' full, that is 24,000 bricks—at their present price about thirty pounds' worth. What am I to do with you?—send you about your business?

Pedersen. Madam, it is the first time—

Leonarda. No, indeed it is not; that is to say, it is certainly the first time the bricks have been burnt, but your accounts have been wrong over and over again, so that I have been led into sending out faulty invoices. What is the matter with you?

Pedersen. Madam, I beg—.

Enter Hans.

Hans. Your horse is saddled, madam, and the General is coming up the avenue.

Leonarda. Very well. (Hans *goes out.*) Have you taken to drink, Pedersen?

47

Pedersen. No, madam.

Leonarda. That wouldn't be like you. But what is it? You look quite changed.—Pedersen! I believe I know! I saw you rowing back across the river last night, from the summer-house in the wood. Are you in love? (PEDERSEN *turns away.*) So that is it. And crossed in love? (*She goes up to him, puts her hand on his shoulder and stands with her back turned to the audience, as he does.*) Are you engaged to her?

Pedersen. Yes.

Leonarda. Then she is not treating you well? She is not true to you? (*Stoops and looks into his face.*) And you love her in spite of it? (*Moves away from him.*) Then you are a weak man, Pedersen. We cannot possibly love those who are false to us. (*Draws on one of her gloves.*) We may suffer horribly for a while; but love them—no!

Pedersen (*still turning away from her*). It is easy for those to talk who have not experienced it.

Leonarda. Experienced it?—You never can tell that. Come to me this evening at seven o'clock.

Pedersen. Yes, madam.

Leonarda. I will talk things over with you then. We will go for a stroll together.

Pedersen. Thank you, madam.

Leonarda. I believe I may be able to help you in your trouble, Pedersen. That is all right—don't think any more about the bricks, or of what I said. Forgive me! (*Holds out her hand to him.*)

Pedersen (*grasping her hand*). Oh, madam!

Enter GENERAL ROSEN.

Rosen. Good morning! (PEDERSEN *crosses the room.*) Bless my soul, Pedersen, you look like a pat of melting

butter! (PEDERSEN *goes out.* ROSEN *turns to* LEONARDA.)
Have you been playing father confessor so early in the
morning, and on such a fine day too? That is too bad.—
By the way, have you heard from Aagot?

Leonarda (putting on her hat). No, I don't know what
has come over the child. It is close on a fortnight since—

Rosen. She is enjoying herself. I remember when I
was enjoying myself I never used to write letters.

Leonarda (looking at him). You were enjoying yourself
last night, I rather think?

Rosen. Do I show it? Dear, dear! I thought that
after a bath and a ride—

Leonarda. This sort of thing cannot go on!

Rosen. You know quite well that if I can't be here I
have to go to my club.

Leonarda. But can't you go to your club without—?
(*Stops, with a gesture of disgust.*)

Rosen. I know what you mean, worse luck. But they
always give one a glass too much.

Leonarda. One glass? Say three!

Rosen. Three, if you like. You know I never was good
at counting.

Leonarda. Well, now you can go for your ride alone.

Rosen. Oh, but—

Leonarda. Yes, I am not going for a ride to-day with a
man who was tipsy last night. (*Takes off her hat.*) Hans!
(HANS *is heard answering her from without.*) Put my
horse up for the present!

Rosen. You are punishing yourself as well as me, you
know. You ought to be out on a day like this—and it is
a sin to deprive the countryside of the pleasure of seeing
you!

Leonarda. Will nothing ever make you take things
seriously?

Rosen. Yes. When the day comes that you are in need of anything, I will be serious.

Leonarda. And you propose to hang about here waiting till I have some ill luck? You will have to wait a long time, I hope. (*Goes to her desk.*)

Rosen. I hope so too!—because meanwhile I shall be able to continue coming here.

Leonarda. Till you get your orders from America.

Rosen. Of course—till I get my orders from Sherman.

Leonarda. You have not had any orders, then?

Rosen. No.

Leonarda. It is beginning to look very suspicious. How long is it since I made you write to him?

Rosen. Oh, I am sure I forget.

Leonarda. It has just struck me—. I suppose you did write?

Rosen. Of course I did. I always do what you tell me.

Leonarda. You stand there twirling your moustache—and when you do that I always know there is some nonsense going on—.

Rosen. How can you suppose such a thing?

Leonarda. You have never written! Why on earth did that never strike me before?

Rosen. I have written repeatedly, I assure you!

Leonarda. But not to Sherman? You have not reported yourself for service again?

Rosen. Do you remember the Russian cigarettes I have so often spoken of? I have got some now. I brought a few with me to try; may I offer you one?

Leonarda. Are you not ashamed to look me in the face?

Rosen. I do everything you tell me—

Leonarda. You have been putting me off with evasions for more than two months—playing a perfect comedy with me! To think that an officer, who has been through

the American war and won honours, rank, and a definite
position, could throw away his time in this way—and in
other ways too—for a whole year now—

Rosen. Excuse me—only eight months.

Leonarda. And isn't that long enough?

Rosen. Too long.   But you know, better than any one,
why I have done it!

Leonarda. Did I ask you to come here?   Do you think
you can tire me out?

Rosen. Leonarda!   (*She looks at him ; he bows formally.*)
I beg your pardon.   Mrs. Falk.

Leonarda. You shall write the letter here, now, and
report yourself for immediate service.

Rosen. If you order me to.

Leonarda. I shall post it.

Rosen. Many thanks.

Leonarda. You are twirling your moustache again.
What are you planning in your mind?

Rosen. I?—Shall I write here?   (*Goes to the desk.*)

Leonarda. Yes.   (*He takes up a pen.*)   Ah, I know what
it is!   As soon as you get home, you will write another
letter recalling this one.

Rosen. Yes, naturally.

Leonarda. Ha, ha, ha!   (*Sits down.*)   Well, I give you
up!

Rosen. Thank you!—Then will you try **one** of my
cigarettes?

Leonarda. No.

Rosen. Nor come for a ride?

Leonarda. No.

Rosen. Am I to come here this evening?

Leonarda. I shall be engaged.

Rosen. But you will be riding to-morrow morning?

Leonarda. I don't know.

Rosen. Then I shall take the liberty of coming to ask. I wish you a very good day.

Leonarda. Look, there is a strange man at the door! (*Gets up.*)

Rosen. What? (*Turns round.*) He? Has he the face to come here? (*Looks out of the open window.*) Pst! Pst!—Hans!—Don't you see my horse has got loose? (*Goes hurriedly out past the stranger, who bows to him.*) Pst! Pst!

Enter HAGBART.

Hagbart. Madam! (*Stops short.*)

Leonarda. May I ask—?

Hagbart. You do not know me, then?

Leonarda. No.

Hagbart. I am Hagbart Tallhaug.

Leonarda. And you dare to tell me so—with a smile on your lips?

Hagbart. If you will only allow me to—

Leonarda. How is it you dare to come here?

Hagbart. If you will only allow me to—

Leonarda. Not a word! Or can there be two men of that name?

Hagbart. No.

Leonarda. So it was you who came forward at the Philharmonic concert, when I was seeking admittance for myself and my adopted daughter, and spoke of me as " a woman of doubtful reputation "? Is that so?

Hagbart. Yes, madam; and I must—

Leonarda (*interrupting him impetuously*). Then get out of here!—Hans! (HANS *is heard answering her from without.*)

Hagbart. Mrs. Falk, first allow me to—.

Enter HANS.

Leonarda. Hans, will you see this gentleman off my premises.

Hans. Certainly, ma'am.

Hagbart. Wait a moment, Hans!

Hans. Shall I, ma'am? (*Looks at* LEONARDA.)

Hagbart. It concerns your niece, Mrs. Falk.

Leonarda. Aagot! Has anything happened to her? I have had no letter from her!

Hagbart. Wait outside, Hans!

Hans (*to* LEONARDA). Shall I, ma'am?

Leonarda. Yes, yes! (HANS *goes out.*) What is it?

Hagbart. No bad news.

Leonarda. But how is it you are here on her behalf?

Hagbart. It is difficult to avoid people at a watering-place, you know—although I must admit your niece did her best. She treated me as contemptuously as possible —even went farther than that; but she could not prevent my talking to people she used to talk to, or my happening to be where she was; so that—well—she heard them talk about me, and heard me talk to them—and in the end she talked to me herself.

Leonarda. Talked to you?

Hagbart. Yes, it is no good denying it—she actually talked to me, and that more than once.

Leonarda. But what is the meaning of this visit to me?

Hagbart. If you will only allow me to—

Leonarda. I want you to deliver your message briefly and concisely—and not a word more than that.

Hagbart. But I cannot do that until you have allowed me to—

Leonarda. Whether you can or not, I shall allow nothing

else. I am not going to give you an excuse for saying that you have been holding conversations with me too.

Hagbart. If you have no objection, I am in love with your niece, Mrs. Falk.

Leonarda. You? With Aagot?—It serves you right!

Hagbart. I know.

Leonarda. Ha, ha! That is how the land lies.

HANS *appears at the open door.*

Hans. Can I go now, ma'am?

Leonarda. Ha, ha!—Yes, you can go. (*Exit* HANS.) Well, what more have you to tell me? Have you given Aagot any hint of this?

Hagbart. Yes.

Leonarda. And what answer did you get?—You are silent. Do you find it difficult to tell me?

Hagbart. I am very glad you take it so well, Mrs. Falk.

Leonarda. Yes, it's funny, isn't it?—Well, what did Aagot say? She generally has plenty to say.

Hagbart. Indeed she has. We came here to-day by the same boat—

Leonarda. By the same boat? Aagot and you? Have you been persecuting her?

Hagbart. Mrs. Falk, you cannot possibly understand if you will not allow me to—

Leonarda. I wish to hear the rest of it from my niece, as I suppose she will be here directly.

Hagbart. Of course, but still—

Leonarda. There will be no more of that sort of thing here! If you intend to persecute my niece with your attentions in the same way as you have persecuted me with your malice, you are at liberty to try. But you shall not come here! I can forbid it here.

Hagbart. But, my dear Mrs. Falk—

Leonarda. I am really beginning to lose my patience, or rather I have lost it already. What have you come here for?

Hagbart. As there is no help for it—well, I will tell you straight out, although it may be a shock to you—I am here to ask for your niece's hand.

Leonarda (*taking up her gloves*). If I were a man, so that there should be nothing " doubtful " about my reply, I would strike you across the face with my gloves.

Hagbart. But you are a woman, so you will not.

Enter HANS.

Hans. Here is Miss Aagot, ma'am.

Aagot (*from without*). Aunt!

Leonarda. Aagot!

Enter AAGOT. HANS *goes out.*

Aagot. Aunt!—That wretched Hans! I was signalling to him—I wanted to surprise you. (*Throws herself into* LEONARDA'S *arms.*)

Leonarda. Child, have you deceived me?

Aagot. Deceived you? I?

Leonarda. I knew it! (*Embraces her.*) Forgive me! I had a moment's horrible doubt—but as soon as I looked at you it was gone!—Welcome, welcome! How pretty you look! Welcome!

Aagot. Oh, aunt!

Leonarda. What is it?

Aagot. You know.

Leonarda. His shameless persecution of you? Yes! (*Meanwhile* HAGBART *has slipped out.*)

Aagot. Hush!—Oh, he has gone!—Have you been cross with him?

Leonarda. Not as cross as he deserved—

Aagot. Didn't I tell him so?

Leonarda (laughing). What did you tell him?

Aagot. How hasty you could be!—Were you really cruel to him?

Leonarda. Do you mean to say you have any sympathy --with him?

Aagot. Have I any—? But, good heavens, hasn't he told you?

Leonarda. What?

Aagot. That he—that I—that we—oh, aunt, don't look so dreadfully at me!—You don't know, then?

Leonarda. No!

Aagot. Heaven help me! Aunt—!

Leonarda. You don't mean to say that you—?

Aagot. Yes, aunt.

Leonarda. With him, who—. In spite of that, you—! Get away from me!

Aagot. Dear, darling aunt, listen to me!

Leonarda. Go away to him! Away with you!

Aagot. Have you looked at him, aunt? Have you seen how handsome he is?

Leonarda. Handsome? He!

Aagot. No, not a bit handsome, of course! Really, you are going too far!

Leonarda. To me he is the man who made a laughing-stock of me in a censorious little town by calling me " a woman of doubtful reputation." And one day he presents himself here as my adopted daughter's lover, and you expect me to think him handsome! You ungrateful child!

Aagot. Aunt!

Leonarda. I have sacrificed eight years of my life—
eight years—in this little hole, stinting myself in every
possible way; and you, for whom I have done this, are
hardly grown up before you fly into the arms of a man
who has covered me with shame. And I am supposed to
put up with it as something quite natural!—and to say
nothing except that I think he is handsome! I—I
won't look at you! Go away!

Aagot (*in tears*). Don't you suppose I have said all that
to myself, a thousand times? That was why I didn't
write. I have been most dreadfully distressed to know
what to do.

Leonarda. At the very first hint of such a thing you
ought to have taken refuge here—with me—if you had had
a scrap of loyalty in you.

Aagot. Aunt! (*Goes on her knees.*) Oh, aunt!

Leonarda. To think you could behave so contemptibly!

Aagot. Aunt!—It was just because he was so sorry for
the way he had behaved to you, that I first—

Leonarda. Sorry? He came here with a smile on his lips!

Aagot. That was because he was in such a fright,
aunt.

Leonarda. Do people smile because they are in a fright?

Aagot. Others don't, but he does. Do you know, dear,
he was just the same with me at first—he smiled and
looked so silly; and afterwards he told me that it was
simply from fright.

Leonarda. If he had felt any qualms of conscience at
all, as you pretend he did, he would at least have taken
the very first opportunity to apologise.

Aagot. Didn't he do that?

Leonarda. No; he stood here beating about the bush
and smiling—

Aagot. Then you must have frightened the sense out of

him, aunt. He is shy, you know.—Aunt, let me tell you
he is studying for the church.

Leonarda. Oh, he is that too, is he!

Aagot. Of course he is. You know he is the bishop's
nephew, and is studying for the church, and of course that
is what made him so prejudiced. But his behaviour that
day was just what opened his eyes—because he is very
kind-hearted. Dear, darling aunt—

Leonarda. Get up! It is silly to lie there like that.
Where did you learn that trick?

Aagot (getting up). I am sure I don't know. But you
frighten me so. (*Cries.*)

Leonarda. I can't help that. You frightened me first,
you know, child.

Aagot. Yes, but it is all quite different from what you
think, aunt. He is no longer our enemy. He has re-
proached himself so genuinely for treating you as he did—
it is perfectly true, aunt. We all heard him say so. He
said so first to other people, so that it should come round
to me; and then I heard him saying so to them; and
eventually he told me so, in so many words.

Leonarda. Why did you not write and tell me?

Aagot. Because you are not like other people, aunt!
If I had as much as mentioned he was there, you would
have told me to come home again at once. You aren't
like others, you know.

Leonarda. But how in the world did it come about that
you—?

Aagot. You know, dear, that if any one sings *your*
praises, that is enough to make me their friend at once.
And when, to crown all, this man did it who had behaved
so unjustly to you, you can well believe that I went
about singing for joy all day. That was the beginning
of it—

Leonarda. Yes, tell me the whole story.

Aagot. That would be simply impossible, aunt! It would take me days!—But I can tell you this, that I had no idea what it was that was upsetting my nerves in such a manner.

Leonarda. If you felt like that, why did you not come away?

Aagot. That was just what I did! But that was also just what made the whole thing happen!

Leonarda. How? Try and tell me a little more calmly and consecutively!

Aagot. Thank you, aunt! It is good of you to listen to me! Good heavens, how I—. (*Bursts into tears.*)

Leonarda. There—there! Tell me all about it from beginning to end.

Aagot. Yes—I was quite feverish for about a week—I thought I was ill—and the others kept asking what was the matter with me. And really I didn't know. There is a whole heap of things I could tell you about those few days—but you wouldn't be able to understand.

Leonarda. Yes, I should.

Aagot. No, you couldn't possibly! I can't, either. I was so wretched then—and now I am so happy—

Leonarda. Well, tell me about it another time. But how did things come to a head?

Aagot. He spoke to me—straight out!

Leonarda. Proposed to you?

Aagot. Yes.—Oh, I feel I am blushing again at the very thought of it.

Leonarda. And you looked foolish?

Aagot. I don't know what I looked like!

Leonarda. What did you do?

Aagot. I gave one scream—a real good scream—and ran; ran home, packed my trunk, and got on board the boat as quick as I could.

Leonarda. And was that all?

Aagot. All? It happened out of doors amongst all the people.

Leonarda. Aagot!

Aagot. It happened so frightfully unexpectedly. I never was so frightened in my life—and so ashamed of myself afterwards. I did nothing but cry on the boat, all the way.

Leonarda. But he must have come by the same boat.

Aagot. Just fancy, he had travelled overland across the promontory and caught the boat on the other side. And I knew nothing about it till I saw him before my eyes! I thought I should sink through the deck. I wanted to run away then, but—oh, aunt, I couldn't! He looked at me with such a wonderful look in his eyes, and took hold of my hands. He spoke to me, but I don't know what he said; everything seemed to be going round and round. And his eyes, aunt! Ah, you haven't looked at them, and that is why you took it so—so—

Leonarda. No, dear.

Aagot. There is something about his mere presence—something so true. And when he looks at me and says—not in words, you know, but still says all the same " I love you so much," I tremble all over. Oh, aunt, kiss me! —There! Thank heaven!—Do you know what he said to-day?

Leonarda. No.

Aagot. That the woman who had fostered—that was the word he used—such a solemn word, but then he is studying for the church—well, that the woman who had fostered such a girl—he meant me, you know—I thought of all my faults, but he will get to know them soon enough—

Leonarda. Well? That the woman who had fostered such a girl as you—

Aagot. —as me, could not have her equal anywhere!

Leonarda. You must have been praising me up nicely?

Aagot. On the contrary. It was afterwards, when he said he would come here first, before me—it was his duty, he said, to stand the first shock. "For heaven's sake don't," I said; "you don't know her, she will crush you!"

Leonarda. Oh, Aagot!

Aagot. It was then that he said, "No, the woman who has fostered such a girl," etcetera, etcetera. Ah, now I see you have been horrid to him.

Leonarda. I had been worried all the morning—and I misunderstood—

Aagot. You shall have no more worries after this. Because people are so kind, you know, and you are going to move about among them again. You, who are so good yourself—

Leonarda. No, that is just what I am not.

Aagot. You? You are only so very difficult to understand, aunt!—Oh, what is it, dear?

Leonarda. I am unhappy, Aagot!

Aagot. Why, aunt? About me?

Leonarda. You are the sunshine of my life; you have brought light and warmth and gentleness into it—but it is just because of that—

Aagot. Because of that? Aunt, I don't understand you.

Leonarda. I am clumsy, I am hard, I am suspicious— wicked. I am a savage, with no more self-restraint than I ever had. What sort of a figure must I cut in his eyes—and in yours? Tell me! Am I not a clumsy, ugly—

Aagot. You are the sweetest woman in the whole world. It is only your indomitable strength and courage and youthfulness—

Leonarda. No, no—tell me the truth! I deserve it! Because, you know, it has been for your sake that for eight years I have only associated with work-people. All that I have will be yours. So have some respect for me, Aagot —tell me the truth! Am I not—what shall I say? Tell me what I am!

Aagot. Adorable!

Leonarda. No, no! I have never realised as strongly as I do now how I have buried myself all these eight years. All the books I have read about the great movements going on in the world outside have not really enlightened me. All that I have read and thought fades away before the first gleam of life that reaches me from the real world of men and women. I see new beauty merely in your new clothes, your fashionable hat—the colours you are wearing—the way they are blended. They mean something that I know nothing of. You bring a fragrance in with you—a breath of freshness; you are so dainty and full of life; whereas everything here has become so old, so heavy, so disjointed—and my life most of all.

Aagot. Well, I must tell you what he said, since you won't believe what I say.

Leonarda. But he knew nothing about me?

Aagot. No—it only indirectly referred to you. He said he had never wanted so much to get to know any one, as he wanted to get to know you, because seeing much of me had made him discover you—that was the very expression he used! And it was an extraordinary chance that—

Leonarda. Stop! I can't bear to think of it!—To think it should be the very man whom we—we—

Aagot. Hated so!—yes, isn't it extraordinary?

Leonarda. The very first time you have been away from me!

Aagot. Yes!

Leonarda. And you come back in a halo of reconciliation and affection for him!

Aagot. But who is responsible for that, I should like to know! And you talk about your life here having made you clumsy and ugly—you, who can manufacture a goddess of victory like me!

Leonarda. No, I don't complain when I see you and hear you—when I have you with me! That is worth paying a price for. It was selfish of me to think for a moment that the price was too high. You are in the springtime of your life—while I—

Aagot. You? What is wrong with your life?

Leonarda. I am beginning to think my life is over.

Aagot. Yours? Your life over? Oh, you pain me by saying such a thing.

Leonarda. I am very happy — very happy about all this! Believe me that is so. But you know—

Aagot. I know how tremendously and incomprehensibly you have changed!

Leonarda. Go, my child—and bring him back!

Aagot. How delicious that sounds! Bring him back! (*Gets up, then stops.*) Thank you, my dear, sweet, darling aunt! (*She runs out.* LEONARDA *falls into a chair by the table and buries her head in her hands.* AAGOT'S *voice is heard without :* "Yes, come along!" *and* HAGBART'S, *answering :* "Is it true?")

Aagot (*coming in with* HAGBART). Come along! (LEO-NARDA *gets up, dries her eyes, and meets them with a smile.*) Aunt, here he is!

Hagbart. Mrs. Falk!

Leonarda. Forgive me!

Hagbart. What?—No, you must forgive me! I haven't been able to ask you to! I—

Aagot. We can talk about that another time! Let aunt look at you now!

Leonarda. You two won't disappoint one another. I can see that.

Aagot. It is wonderfully sweet of you, aunt!

Leonarda. Yes, love one another! Bring some beauty, some warmth, some colour into this cold house!

Aagot. Oh, aunt—!

Leonarda. Have you kissed her yet? (Aagot *moves a little away from* Hagbart.) Go on! (*They embrace.*)

Aagot (*running from him to* Leonarda). But, dearest aunt, are you crying?

Leonarda. Don't bother about me!—Have you told your uncle, the bishop, about it?

Hagbart. Not yet.

Leonarda. You haven't?—Well, you have the worst of it before you yet, I am afraid.

Hagbart. No; now that I have got as far as this, nothing shall stand in my way!

Aagot. Do you hear that, aunt?

Curtain.

ACT II

(Scene.—*A room in the* Bishop's *house, some weeks later.
A door at the back of the room leads to another large
room. Another door in the right-hand wall ; windows
in the left. Well forward, by one of the windows, a
large easy-chair. Farther back, a writing-desk and
chair. On the right, near the door, a couch, and chairs
ranged along the wall. Chairs also alongside the
door at the back. The* Bishop *is sitting on the couch,
talking to* Hagbart.)

Bishop. My dear Hagbart, you keep on telling me that
you have acted up to your convictions. Very well, do
you want to forbid my acting up to mine?

Hagbart. You know that all I ask, uncle, is that you
will see her and talk to her first.

Bishop. But if that is exactly what I don't wish to do?
You have made things difficult for us, you know, by
choosing a wife out of your own class—although at the
same time we have grown fonder of her every day, and
are ready to do anything for *her.* But farther than that
we cannot go. Do you want to read my letter?

Hagbart. No.

Bishop. I think you should. It is quite a polite letter.

Hagbart. I know you can put things politely enough.
But it is the fact, uncle—the fact of your doing it!

Bishop. Yes—I cannot alter that.

Hagbart. Could you not at all events postpone sending
the letter?

Bishop. It is sent.

Hagbart. Sent?

Bishop. This morning. Yes. So there is nothing more to be done.

Hagbart. Uncle, you are cruel!

Bishop. How can you say that, Hagbart? I have acquiesced in your giving up your clerical career—and Heaven alone knows what a grief that is to me. (*Gets up.*) But I will not acquiesce in your bringing into my house a woman who does not even bear her husband's name. Do we as much as know who her husband was? She was both married and divorced abroad. And we don't know anything more about her life since then; it is scarcely likely it has been blameless. Since she came here she has never once been to church. She has led a most eccentric life, and lately has been allowing a man of very evil reputation to visit her.

Hagbart. General Rosen?

Bishop. Yes, General Rosen. He is next door to a drunkard. And he is a dissolute fellow in other ways, too.

Hagbart. He goes everywhere, all the same. He even comes here.

Bishop. Well, you see, he distinguished himself on military service; he has many sociable qualities, and he is well connected. It is the way of the world.

Hagbart. But Mrs. Falk is not to be received?

Bishop. She is a woman.

Hagbart. How long will this sort of thing be endured?

Bishop. Come, come—are you getting those ideas into your head too? You seem to have imbibed a lot of new doctrines lately!

Hagbart. You should have seen her and talked to her once at least, before making up your mind.

Bishop. I will tell you something in confidence, Hagbart. Justice Röst, who lives out there in the country, has often

seen General Rosen coming away from her house at most
unseemly hours.   I will have nothing to do with women
of that sort.

Hagbart. What about men of that sort?

Bishop. Well, as I said, that is quite another matter.

Hagbart. Quite so.—Mrs. Falk takes compassion on
the General; she interests herself in him.   That is all.

Bishop. Did she know him previously, then?

Hagbart. Very likely.

Bishop. Then she has her own private reasons for acting
as she does.

Hagbart. Shall I tell you what it is?   She has a kinder
heart than any of us, and can make a sacrifice more
willingly.

Bishop. So you know that?

Hagbart. Yes.   Hers is a finer nature than any of
ours; it is more completely developed, intellectually and
morally.

Bishop. I am listening to you with the profoundest
amazement!

Hagbart. Oh, don't misunderstand me!   She has her
faults.

Bishop. Really, you admit that!—I want to beg something of you earnestly, Hagbart.   Go away for a little
while.

Hagbart. Go away!

Bishop. Yes, to your uncle's, for instance.   Only for a
week or a fortnight.   You need to clear your thoughts,
badly—about all sorts of things.   Your brain is in a
whirl.

Hagbart. That is true; but—

Bishop. Speak out!

Hagbart. My brain has been in a whirl much longer
than you have had any idea of.   It has been so ever since

that day in winter when I did Mrs. Falk such a horrible
injustice.

Bishop. Not exactly an injustice, but—

Hagbart. Yes, an injustice! It was a turning point in
my life. To think that I should have given way to such
a fanatical outburst! It ended in my being terrified at
myself—well, I won't bore you with the whole story of
my long fight with myself. You saw nothing of it,
because I was not here. But at last, when I got ill and
had to go away and take the waters, and then happened
to see Aagot—the effect on me was more than anything
I could have imagined. I seemed to see the truth; man-
kind seemed different, and I seemed to hear the voice of
life itself at last. You cannot imagine the upheaval it
caused in me. It must be that she had something within
her that I lacked, and had always lacked! It was her
wonderful naturalness; everything she did was done with
more charm and gaiety than I found in any one else, and
she was quite unconscious of it herself. I used to ask
myself what was the reason of it—how it could be that it
had been her lot to grow up so free and wholesome. I
realised that it was because I had been oblivious to what
I lacked myself, that I had been so fanatically severe upon
others. I know it is humiliating to confess it, but it is
true. I have always been blundering and impetuous.—
But what was I going to say?

Bishop. You were going to speak about Mrs. Falk, I
presume.

Hagbart. Yes!—My dear uncle, don't take it amiss.
But all this time I have never been able to keep away
from her.

Bishop. Then it is she you have been talking to?

Hagbart. Of course!—and of course, that is to say, to
Aagot too. You propose my going away. I cannot! If

I could multiply myself by two, or if I could double the length of the days, I should never have enough of being with her! No, I have seen daylight now. On no account can I go away.

Bishop. And you call that seeing daylight! Poor boy!

Hagbart. I cannot discuss it with you. You would no more understand than you did that day when you took away those books of grandmother's from me and put them in the lumber-room.

Bishop. Oh, you are bringing that up again? Well, you are at liberty to do as you please. You shall not have the right to say I have exercised any compulsion.

Hagbart. No, uncle, you are very good—to me.

Bishop. But there is a new fact to be taken into consideration. I have noticed it for some days.

Hagbart. What do you mean?

Bishop. In all this conversation we have just had, you have only mentioned Aagot's name twice, at most.

Hagbart. But we were not talking about Aagot.

Bishop. Are you not in love with her any longer?

Hagbart. Not in love with Aagot? (*Laughs.*) Can you ask that? Do you mean to say—?

Bishop. Yes, I mean to say—

Hagbart (*laughing again*). No, that is quite a misunderstanding on your part, uncle.

Bishop. Well, I say it again: go away for a week or a fortnight, Hagbart! Consider the situation from a distance—both your own position and that of others!

Hagbart. It is impossible, absolutely impossible, uncle. It would be just as useful to say to me: " Lie down and go to sleep for a week or a fortnight, Hagbart; it will do you good "! No. All my faculties are awake at last— yes, at last—so much so, that sometimes I can scarcely control myself.

Bishop. That is the very reason.

Hagbart. The very reason why I must go straight ahead, for once in my life! No, I must stay here now. —Well, good morning, uncle! I must go out for a turn.

Bishop. Go to call on Mrs. Falk, you mean.

Hagbart (*laughing*). Unfortunately I haven't the face to do that till this afternoon; I was there the whole day yesterday. But our conversation has set all my thoughts agog again, and when I have no means of appeasing them I have to go out and walk. Thank you, uncle, for being so indulgent to me!

Bishop. Then you don't wish to read my letter?

Hagbart. Ah, that is true—the letter! That upsets the whole thing again. I don't know how I came to forget that.

Bishop. You see for yourself how confused and distracted you are. You need to pull yourself together. Go away for a little!

Hagbart. It is impossible!—Good-bye, uncle!

Bishop. Here is grandmother!

Enter the GRANDMOTHER *and* CORNELIA.

Hagbart. Good morning, grandmother! Have you slept well?

Grandmother (*coming forward on* CORNELIA'S *arm*). Excellently!

Cornelia. She slept well into the morning.

Bishop. I am delighted, grandmother. (*Takes her other arm.*)

Grandmother. You needn't shout so loud. It is a fine day to-day and I can hear very well. (*To* HAGBART.) You didn't come in to see me last night.

Hagbart. I came in too late, grandmother.

Grandmother. I tell you, you needn't talk so loud.

Cornelia. She always wants to make out that she can hear.

Grandmother (*as they settle her in the big chair by the window*). This is a nice seat—

Bishop. And I am always delighted to see you sitting there.

Grandmother. The window — and the mirror over there.

Cornelia. Yes, it enables you to see everything.

Grandmother. How you do shout, all you good people!

Bishop. I must go and change my things, if you will excuse me. (*Goes out to the right.*)

Cornelia. Do you want anything more?

Grandmother. No, thank you. (CORNELIA *goes out at the back.*)

Hagbart. Dear, good grandmother! You are the only one here who understands me!

Grandmother (*trying to look round the room*). Are we alone?

Hagbart. Yes.

Grandmother. Has your uncle called on Mrs. Falk?

Hagbart. No, worse luck; he has written her a letter.

Grandmother. I thought as much.

Hagbart. Isn't it shameful, grandmother! He won't see her once, or talk to her, before judging her.

Grandmother. They are all alike, these—. Are we alone?

Hagbart. Yes, grandmother.

Grandmother. You must have patience, Hagbart! You used to be patient.

Hagbart. Yes, grandmother.

Grandmother. I have seen so many generations — so

many different ways of behaving. In my day we were tolerant.

Hagbart. I enjoyed reading your books so much, grand-mother!

Grandmother. Of course you did.—Are we alone?

Hagbart. Yes, grandmother.

Grandmother. I am quite in love with your *fiancée*, Hagbart. She is like what girls were in my day.

Hagbart. Courageous, weren't they?

Grandmother. Yes, and independent. They seem quite different nowadays.—Are we alone?

Hagbart. Yes.

Grandmother. You get married—and I will come and live with you and her. Hush!

Hagbart. Do you mean it?

Grandmother. Hush! (*Looks out of the window.*) There is Justice Röst coming, with his wife. Go and tell your uncle!

Hagbart. Yes.

Grandmother. I might have expected it. They came up from the country yesterday.

Hagbart. Good-bye, then, grandmother!

Grandmother. Good-bye, my boy! (HAGBART *goes out to the right. The door at the back is opened.* CORNELIA *ushers in* RÖST *and* MRS. RÖST.)

Cornelia. Please walk in!

Mrs. Röst. Thank you! You must excuse us for calling so early. We came up from the country yesterday, and my husband has to go to the courts for a little while!

Röst. I have to go to the courts to-day. (*The* BISHOP *comes in from the right.*)

Bishop. Welcome!

Röst and Mrs. Röst. Thank you!

Mrs. Röst. You must excuse our calling so early; but

we came up from the country yesterday, and my husband
has to go to the courts to-day.

Röst. I have to go to the courts for a little while.

Bishop. I know.

Mrs. Röst. And there is the old lady in her chair
already!

Röst. Good morning, my dear madam!

Mrs. Röst. Good morning!—No, please don't get up!

Grandmother. Oh, I can get up still.

Röst. Ah, I wish I were as active as you!

Mrs. Röst. My husband was saying to Miss Cornelia only
last night—

Grandmother. You need not strain yourself so. I can
hear perfectly well. (*The others exchange glances.*)

Röst. I was saying to Miss Cornelia only last night—
we met for a few moments after the service—

Grandmother. I know, I know.

Röst. I said I had never known any one of over ninety
have all their faculties so remarkably clear—

Mrs. Röst. —so remarkably clear as yours! And such
good health, too! My husband has suffered a great deal
from asthma lately.

Röst. I have suffered a great deal from asthma
lately.

Mrs. Röst. And I from a heart trouble, which—

Grandmother. We did not know anything about such
ailments in my day.

Mrs. Röst. Isn't she sweet! She doesn't remember that
people were sometimes ill in her day.

Bishop. Lovely weather we are having!

Röst. Delightful weather! I cannot in the least understand how it is that I—. (*The* BISHOP *brings a chair
forward for him.*) Oh, please don't trouble, my lord!
Allow me.

Mrs. Röst. My husband must have caught cold. (RÖST *sits down.*)

Cornelia. It certainly was draughty in church last night.

Röst. But we sat in the corner farthest from the door.

Mrs. Röst. We sat in the corner farthest from the door. That was why we were not able to bid your lordship good evening afterwards.

Bishop. There was such a crowd.

Röst, Mrs. Röst, and Cornelia. Such a crowd!

Mrs. Röst. These services must be a great help in your lordship's labours.

Röst. Yes, every one says that.

Bishop. Yes, if only the result were something a little more practical. We live in sad times.

All three (*as before*). Sad times!

Mrs. Röst. We only just heard yesterday—and we met so many friends that I was prevented from asking your sister about it—we have only just heard—

Röst. And that is why we have come here to-day. We believe in being straightforward!

Mrs. Röst. Straightforward! That **is my** husband's motto.

Bishop. Probably you mean about Hagbart's engagement?

Röst and Mrs. Röst. To Miss Falk?

Cornelia. Yes, it is quite true.

Mrs. Röst. Really?

Cornelia. My brother came to the conclusion that he had no right to oppose it.

Röst. Quite so. It must have been a difficult matter for your lordship to decide.

Bishop. I cannot deny that it was.

Mrs. Röst. How Mr. Tallhaug has changed!

Röst. Yes, it seems only the other day he—

Bishop. We must not be too severe on young people in that respect nowadays, Mrs. Röst.

Röst. It is the spirit of the time!

Bishop. Besides, I must say that the young lady is by no means displeasing to me.

Cornelia. My brother has a very good opinion of her—although he finds her manner perhaps a little free, a little too impetuous.

Mrs. Röst. But her adoptive mother?

Röst. Yes, her adoptive mother!

Cornelia. My brother has decided not to call on her.

Röst and Mrs. Röst. Really!

Mrs. Röst. We are extremely glad to hear that!

Röst. It was what we wanted to know! Everybody we met yesterday was anxious to know.

Mrs. Röst. Everybody! We were so concerned about it.

Cornelia. My brother has written to her, to make it quite clear to her.

Röst. Naturally!

Mrs. Röst. We are very glad to hear it!

Grandmother (*looking out of the window*). There is a carriage stopping at the door.

Cornelia. I thought I heard a carriage, too. (*Gets up.*)

Grandmother. There is a lady getting out of it.

Mrs. Röst. A lady?—Good heavens, surely it is not—? (*Gets up.*)

Röst. What do you say? (*Gets up.*)

Cornelia. She has a veil on.

Mrs. Röst. I really believe—! (*To her husband.*) You look, my dear—you know her.

Röst. It is she; I recognise her coachman Hans.

Bishop (*who has got up*). But perhaps it is Miss Aagot?

Cornelia. No, it is not Miss Aagot.—She is in the house by this time. What are we to do?

Mrs. Röst. Has she not had your lordship's letter?

Bishop. Yes, this morning.

Röst. And in spite of that—?

Bishop. Perhaps for that very reason. Ahem!—Cornelia, you must go down and—

Cornelia. Not on any account! I refuse!

Mrs. Röst (*to her husband*). Come, dear! Be quick, let us get away. (*Looks for her parasol.*) Where is my parasol?

Bishop (*in a low voice*). Won't you wait a little while, Mr. Röst?

Röst. Oho!

Mrs. Röst. My parasol! I can't find my parasol.

Röst. Because you have got it in your hand, my love!

Mrs. Röst. So I have! You see how upset I am. Make haste—come along! Can we get out this way?

Röst. Through the Bishop's bedroom!

Mrs. Röst. Oh!—But if you come with me, my dear!—Are we to meet this woman? Why do you stand still? Surely you don't want to—?

Röst. Let us wait a little.

Mrs. Röst. Wait? So that you may talk to her? Oh, you men—you are all alike!

Bishop. But, you know, some one must—. Cornelia!

Cornelia. Not for worlds! I am not going to stir an inch.

Grandmother. Gracchus!

Bishop. Yes, grandmother?

Mrs. Röst. Now the old lady is going to interfere. I thought as much!

Grandmother. Courtesy is a duty that every one must recognise.

Bishop. You are quite right. (*Goes towards the back of the room ; at the same time a knock is heard on the door*). Come in! (*The door opens, and* LEONARDA *enters.*)

Mrs. Röst. It is she!

Röst. Be quiet!

Mrs. Röst. But wouldn't you rather—?

Leonarda. Excuse me, am I speaking to the Bishop?

Bishop. Yes, madam. Whom have I the honour to—?

Leonarda. Mrs. Falk.

Bishop. Allow me to introduce my sister—and Mr. Justice Röst and Mrs. Röst—and this is—

Leonarda. " Grandmamma " of whom I have heard, I think!

Bishop. Yes. Let me present Mrs. Falk to you, grandmother.

Grandmother (*getting up*). I am very glad to see you, ma'am.

Mrs. Röst and Cornelia. What does she say?

Grandmother. As the oldest of the family—which is the only merit I possess—let me bid you welcome. (LEONARDA *gives a start, then kneels down and kisses her hand.*)

Mrs. Röst. Good gracious!

Cornelia. Well!

Mrs. Röst. Let us go away!

Röst (*in a low voice*). Does your lordship wish—?

Bishop (*in the same tone*). No, thank you—I must go through with it now.

Röst. Good morning, then!

Bishop. Many thanks for your visit and for being so frank with me.

Mrs. Röst. That is always our way, your lordship. Good morning!

Cornelia (*as they advance to take leave of her*). I will see you out.

Röst (to the GRANDMOTHER). I hope I shall always see you looking as well, madam!

Mrs. Röst. Good-bye, madam! No, please don't disturb yourself. You have over-exerted yourself just now, you know.

Grandmother. The same to you.

Röst and Mrs. Röst. I beg your pardon?

Bishop. She thought you were wishing her good day— or something of that sort.

Röst and Mrs. Röst. Oh, I see! (*They laugh. They bow ceremoniously in silence to* LEONARDA *as they pass her ;* CORNELIA *and the* BISHOP *go with them to see them out, the* BISHOP *turning at the door and coming back into the room.*)

Bishop (to LEONARDA). Won't you sit down?

Leonarda. Your lordship sent me a letter to-day. (*She pauses for an answer, but without effect.*) In it you give me to understand, as politely as possible, that your family does not wish to have any intercourse with me.

Bishop. I imagined, Mrs. Falk, that you had no such desire, either previously or now.

Leonarda. What it really means is that you want me to make over my property to the two young people, and disappear.

Bishop. If you choose to interpret it in that way, Mrs. Falk.

Leonarda. I presume your nephew has told you that my means are not such as to allow of my providing for one establishment here and another for myself elsewhere.

Bishop. Quite so. But could you not sell your property?

Leonarda. And all three of us leave here, your lordship means? Of course that would be possible; but the property is just now becoming of some value, because of the projected railway—and, besides, it has been so long in our family.

Bishop. It is a very fine property.

Leonarda. And very dear to us.

Bishop. It pains me deeply that things should have taken this turn.

Leonarda. Then may I not hope that the fact may influence your lordship's decision in some degree?

Bishop. My decision, madam, has nothing to do with your property.

Leonarda. During all these eight years have I offended you in any way—or any one here?

Bishop. Mrs. Falk, you know quite well that you have not.

Leonarda. Or is it on account of the way I have brought up my niece—?

Bishop. Your niece does you the greatest credit, madam.

Leonarda. Then perhaps some of my people have been laying complaints about me?—or some one has been complaining of them?

Bishop. Not even the most censorious person, my dear madam, could pretend that you have been anything but exemplary in that respect.

Leonarda. Then what is it?

Bishop. You can scarcely expect me to tell a lady—

Leonarda. I will help you out. It is my past life.

Bishop. Since you say it yourself—yes.

Leonarda. Do you consider that nothing can expiate a past—about which, moreover, you know nothing?

Bishop. I have not seen in you any signs of a desire to expiate it, Mrs. Falk.

Leonarda. You mean that you have not seen me at confession or in church?

Bishop. Yes.

Leonarda. Do you want me to seek expiation by being untrue to myself?

Bishop. No; but the way I refer to is the only sure one.

Leonarda. There are others. I have chosen the way of hard work and duty.

Bishop. I said the only sure way, Mrs. Falk. Your way does not protect against temptation.

Leonarda. You have something definite in your mind when you say that, have you not?—Shall I help you out again? It is General Rosen.

Bishop. Precisely.

Leonarda. You think I ought to send him away?

Bishop. Yes.

Leonarda. But it would be all up with him if I did. And there is a good deal of ability in him.

Bishop. I have neither the right nor the desire to meddle in affairs I know nothing of; but I must say that only a person of unimpeachable reputation should attempt the rescue of such a man as General Rosen.

Leonarda. You are quite right.

Bishop. You are paying too high a price for it, Mrs. Falk, and without any certainty of achieving anything.

Leonarda. Maybe. But there is one aspect of the matter that you have forgotten.

Bishop. And that is?

Leonarda. Compassion.

Bishop. Quite so.—Yes.—Of course, if you approach the matter from that point of view, I have nothing to say.

Leonarda. You don't believe it?

Bishop. I only wish the matter depended upon what I myself believe. But it does not, Mrs. Falk.

Leonarda. But surely you will admit that one ought to do good even at the risk of one's reputation?

Bishop. Undoubtedly.

Leonarda. Well, will your lordship not apply that maxim to yourself? It is quite possible that for a while your congregation's faith in you might be a little disturbed if you were to call upon me; but you know now, from my own lips, that the rumours you have heard are false, and that you ought rather to be all the more anxious to support me in what I am trying to do. And in that way you will do a good turn to these two young people, and to me, without driving me away. For some years now I have lived only for others. One does not do that without making some sacrifices, my lord—especially when, as in my case, one does not feel that one's life is quite over.

Bishop. You look the picture of youth, Mrs. Falk!

Leonarda. Oh, no—still I have not done it without a struggle. And now I want a little reward for it. Who would not? I want to spend my life with those for whom I have sacrificed myself; I want to see their happiness and make it mine. Do not rob me of that, my lord! It depends upon you!

Bishop. I do not quite see how it depends upon me.

Leonarda. It depends upon you for this reason; if my exile is to be the price paid for her marriage, my niece will never consent to wed your nephew.

Bishop. That would be very distressing to me, Mrs. Falk.

Leonarda. I made haste to come to you, before she should know anything about it. I have brought your letter with me. Take it back, my lord! (*Searches in her pocket for the letter.*)

Bishop (*noticing her growing anxiety*). What is wrong?

Leonarda. The letter!—I laid it on my desk while I dressed to come out, meaning to bring it with me—but in my hurry and anxiety I have forgotten it! And now

F

Aagot is making out accounts at that very desk. If she sees your handwriting she will suspect something at once, because of course we have been expecting you every day.

Bishop. Well, I suppose there is nothing to be done?

Leonarda. Indeed there is. When she comes here—for she will understand everything and come straight here— could not your lordship meet her yourself, and say to her—. (*Stops short.*)

Bishop. Say what?

Leonarda. " I have been mistaken. People should be judged, not by their mistakes, but by what they have achieved; not by their beliefs, but by their efforts towards goodness and truth. I mean to teach my congregation that lesson by calling upon your aunt next Sunday." (*The* GRANDMOTHER *nods at her approvingly.* LEONARDA *sees this, takes her hand, and turns again towards the* BISHOP.) This venerable lady pleads for me too. She belongs to a day that was more tolerant than ours—at all events than ours is in this little out-of-the-way place. All the wisdom of her long life is summed up in these two words: Have forbearance!

Bishop. There is one kind of forbearance, Mrs. Falk, that is forbidden us—the forbearance that would efface the distinction between good and evil. That is what the " toleration " of my grandmother's day meant; but it is not an example to be followed.

Leonarda (*leaving the* GRANDMOTHER'S *side*). If I have erred—if I seem of no account, from the lofty standpoint from which you look upon life—remember that you serve One who was the friend of sinners.

Bishop. I will be your friend when I see you seeking your soul's salvation. I will do all I can then.

Leonarda. Help me to expiate my past! That means everything to me—and is not much for you to do. I only

ask for a little show of courtesy, instead of indignities! I
will contrive that we shall seldom meet. Only don't
drive me away — because that means exposing me to
contempt. Believe me, I will give you no cause for shame;
and your good deed will be rewarded by the gratitude of
the young people.

Bishop. I am deeply distressed at having to take up this
attitude towards you. You are bound to think me hard-
hearted; but that is not the case. I have to consider that
I am the guardian of thousands of anxious consciences.
I dare not for my nephew's sake offend the respect they
feel for me, the trust they put in me; nor dare I disregard
the law we all must follow. For a bishop to do as I have
done in opening my doors to your niece, is in itself no
small thing, when you consider the dissensions that are
going on in the Church nowadays. I cannot, I dare not,
go farther and open my doors to a woman whom my whole
congregation—albeit unjustly—well, I won't wound your
feelings by going on.

Leonarda. Really?

Bishop. Believe me, it gives me great pain. You have
made a remarkable impression upon me personally.
(*Meanwhile the* GRANDMOTHER *has got up to go out of the
room.*)

Leonarda. Are you going away? (*The* BISHOP *goes to
the wall and rings a bell.*)

Grandmother. Yes—I am too old for these scenes. And,
after what I have just heard, I am sure I have no right
to sit here either. (CORNELIA *comes in, takes her arm, and
assists her out.*)

Leonarda (*coming forward*). Now I can say this to your
lordship: you have no courage. Standing face to face
with me here, you know what you ought to do, but dare
not do it.

Bishop. You are a woman—so I will not answer.

Leonarda. It is because I am a woman that you have said things to me to-day that you would not have said to —to General Rosen, for instance—a man who is allowed to come to your lordship's house in spite of his past life, and his present life too.

Bishop. He shall come here no more in future. Besides, you cannot deny that there is a difference between your two cases.

Leonarda. There is indeed a difference; but I did not expect the distinction to be made on these lines. Nor did I imagine, my lord, that your duty was to protect, not the weaker vessel, but the stronger—to countenance open vice, and refuse help to those who are unjustly accused!

Bishop. Do you think there is any use in our prolonging this conversation?

AAGOT *opens the door at the back and calls from the doorway.*

Aagot. Aunt!

Leonarda. Aagot! Good heavens!

Aagot (*coming forward*). Aunt!

Leonarda. Then you know? (AAGOT *throws herself into her arms.*) My child!

Aagot. I felt sure you would be here, heaven help me!

Leonarda. Control yourself, my child!

Aagot. No, I cannot. This is too much.

Bishop. Would you ladies rather be alone?

Aagot. Where is Hagbart?

Bishop. He has gone out for a walk.

Aagot. It makes me boil with rage! So this was to be the price of my being received into your family—that I was to sell the one who has been a mother to me! Sell her, whom I love and honour more than all the world!

Bishop. Mrs. Falk, do you wish to continue?—or—

Aagot. Continue what? Your negotiations for the sale of my dear one? No. And if it were a question of being admitted to heaven without her, I should refuse!

Bishop. Child! Child!

Aagot. You must let me speak! I must say what is in my heart. And this, at any rate, is in it—that I hold fast to those I love, with all the strength that is in my being!

Bishop. You are young, and speak with the exaggeration of youth. But I think we should do better to put an end to this interview; it can lead to nothing.

Leonarda. Let us go.

HAGBART *appears at the door.*

Aagot (seeing him before the others). Hagbart!

Hagbart. I heard your voice from outside. Mrs. Falk—

Aagot. Hagbart! (*She goes towards him, but as he hastens to her side she draws back.*) No—don't touch me!

Hagbart. But, Aagot—?

Aagot. Why did you not manage to prevent this? You never said a word to me about it!

Hagbart. Because really I knew nothing about it.

Aagot. One becomes conscious of such things as that without needing to be told. It hasn't weighed much on your mind!—Did you not know of it just now?

Hagbart. Yes, but—

Aagot. And you didn't fly to tell us?

Hagbart. It is true I—

Aagot. Your mind was taken up with something else altogether. And my only aim in life has been that everything should be made right for her! I thought you were going to do that.

Hagbart. You are unjust, Aagot. What can I do—?

Aagot. No, you are too much of a dreamer. But this you must realise—that I am not going to buy an honoured position at the price of insults to my aunt; that is the very last thing possible.

Hagbart. Of course! But need there be any question of that? I will come and live with you two, and—

Aagot. You talk like a fool!

Leonarda. Aagot! Aagot!

Aagot. Oh, I feel so hurt, so deceived, so mortified—I must say it out. Because to-day is not the first of it— nor is this the only thing.

Leonarda. No, I can understand that. But what is it? You are wounding his love for you.

Aagot (*bitterly*). His love for me!

Leonarda. Are you out of your mind? You are talking wildly!

Aagot. No, I am only telling the truth!

Leonarda (*earnestly, and lowering her voice*). Angry words, Aagot? You, who have seen into the bottom of his heart in quiet sacred moments! You who know how true, how stedfast he is! He is different from other men, Aagot—

Aagot (*drawing away from her*). Stop! stop! You don't see!

Leonarda. You are out of your senses, my child! Your behaviour is disgracing us.

Aagot. The greatest disgrace is his, then—because it is not me he loves! (*Bursts into tears and rushes to the back of the room.*)

Bishop (*to* HAGBART, *in a low voice*). I hope now you will go away for a little while.

Hagbart. Yes.

Bishop. Come away, then. (*Goes out to the left,* HAG-BART *follows him.*)

Aagot (*coming forward to* LEONARDA). Can you forgive me?

Leonarda. Let us go home.

Aagot. But say something kind to me.

Leonarda. No.

Aagot. I won't let you go away till you do.

Leonarda. I cannot.

Aagot. Aunt, I am not jealous of you.

Leonarda. Be quiet!

Aagot. Only you must let me go away for a few days—I must get things straight in my mind. (*Bursts into tears.*) Oh, aunt—for pity's sake—do you love him? (LEONARDA *tries to get away from her.*) I don't love him any longer! If you love him, aunt, I will give him up!

Leonarda. At least hold your tongue about it, here in another person's house!—If you are not coming with me, I am going home by myself.

Aagot. Then I shall never follow you.

Leonarda. You are completely out of your senses!

Aagot. Yes; I cannot live, unless you speak to me gently and look at me kindly.—God keep you, aunt, now and always!

Leonarda (*turning to her*). My child!

Aagot. Ah! (*Throws herself into her arms.*)

Leonarda. Let us go home!

Aagot. Yes.

Curtain.

ACT III

(SCENE.—*The garden at* LEONARDA FALK'S *house some
days later. On the left, a summer-house with table and
chairs. A large basket, half full of apples, is on the
table.* LEONARDA *is standing talking to* PEDERSEN.)

Leonarda. Very well, Pedersen; if the horses are not
needed here, we may as well send to fetch Miss Aagot
home. Can we send to-day?

Pedersen. Certainly, ma'am.

Leonarda. Then please send Hans as soon as possible
with a pair of horses to the hill farm for her. It is too
cold for her to be up there now, anyway.

Pedersen. I will do so. (*Turns to go.*)

Leonarda. By the way, Pedersen, how has that little
affair of yours been going?

Pedersen. Oh—

Leonarda. Come to me this evening. We will see if we
can continue our little talk about it.

Pedersen. I have been wishing for that for a long time,
ma'am.

Leonarda. Yes, for the last eight or ten days I have not
been able to think of anything properly.

Pedersen. We have all noticed that there has been
something wrong with you, ma'am.

Leonarda. We all have our troubles. (PEDERSEN *waits ;
but as* LEONARDA *begins to pick apples carefully from a
young tree and put them in a small basket that is on her arm,
he goes out to the left.* HAGBART *appears from the right,
and stands for a minute without her seeing him.*)

Hagbart. Mrs. Falk! (LEONARDA *gives a little scream.*)
I beg your pardon, but I have been looking for you everywhere. How are you? I have only just this moment
got back.

Leonarda. Aagot is not at home.

Hagbart. I know. Has she been away the whole
time?

Leonarda. Yes.

Hagbart. Will she be away long?

Leonarda. I am sending the horses up to-day, so she
should be here by the day after to-morrow.

Hagbart. It was you I wanted to speak to, Mrs. Falk.

Leonarda. About Aagot?

Hagbart. Yes, about Aagot—amongst other things.

Leonarda. But couldn't you wait—till some other time?

Hagbart. Mrs. Falk, I came straight here from the
steamer; so you can see for yourself—

Leonarda. But if it concerns Aagot, and she is not here?

Hagbart. The part of it that concerns Aagot is soon
said. She was perfectly right—only I did not know it at
the time.

Leonarda. Good God!

Hagbart. I do not love Aagot.

Leonarda. But if Aagot loves you?

Hagbart. She has showed me lately that she does not.
Did she not tell you so, plainly?

Leonarda. She was—how shall I put it?—too excited
for me to attach much importance to what she said.

Hagbart. Then she did tell you so. I thought she had
—indeed I was sure of it. Aagot does not love me, but
she loves you. She wants you to be happy.

Leonarda. If you do not love Aagot, it seems to me you
ought not to have come here.

Hagbart. Perhaps you are right. But I am not the

same man as I was when I used to come here before; nor do I come for the same reason.

Leonarda. If you do not love Aagot, I must repeat that you have no right to be here. You owe that much consideration both to her and to me.

Hagbart. I assure you that it is from nothing but the sincerest consideration for you that I am here now.

Leonarda (who up to this point has been standing by the tree). Then I must go!

Hagbart. You won't do that!

Leonarda. You seem to me completely changed.

Hagbart. Thank goodness for that!—because I don't feel any great respect for the man I was before. Many people can decide such things in a moment, but it has taken me time to see my course clearly.

Leonarda. I don't understand you.

Hagbart (almost before the words are out of her mouth, coming close to her). You do understand me!

Leonarda. It would be wicked! Take care!

Hagbart. Your hand is trembling—

Leonarda. That is not true!

Hagbart. They say there is a devil in every one that should not be waked. It is a foolish saying, because these devils are our vital forces.

Leonarda. But we ought to have them under control. That is the lesson my life has taught me; it has cost me dear, and I mean to profit by it.

Hagbart. If I did not believe that it was the impulse of truth itself that guided me to you, I should not be standing here. I have had a long struggle. I have had to give up one prejudice after another, to enable my soul to find itself fully and go forward confidently. It has brought me to you—and now we will go forward together.

Leonarda. That might have been, without this.

Hagbart. I love you! It is you I have loved in her—since the very first day. I love you!

Leonarda. Then have respect for me—and go!

Hagbart. Leonarda!

Leonarda. No, no! (*Shrinks away from him.*) Oh, why did this happen?

Hagbart. It has come upon us step by step. The cruel obstacles in our way have only proved friends to us, in bringing us together. Give yourself up to happiness, as I do now!

Leonarda. I do not deserve happiness. I have never expected that.

Hagbart. I don't know what you have gone through to make you what you are now—so beautiful, so good, so true; but this I do know, that if the others had not judged you by your failures, I should not have loved you for what you have achieved. And I thought that might give me some value in your eyes.

Leonarda. Thank you for that, from my heart!—But the world disapproves of such things. It disapproves of a young man's making love to an older woman, and if—

Hagbart. I have never cared much about the world's opinion, even in the days when I was most hidebound in prejudice. It is your opinion I want—yours only!

Leonarda. And my answer is that one who is alone can get along without the world's sympathy—but it is different with a couple. They will soon feel the cold wind of the world's displeasure blowing between them.

Hagbart. When you answer me, it makes what I have said seem so formal and ceremonious—so clumsy. But I must just be as I am; I cannot alter myself. Dearest, from the moment I felt certain that it was you I loved, only one thing seemed of any importance to me—everything else was blotted out. And that is why I do not understand what you say. Do you suppose they will try to make me tire of you? Do you suppose that is possible?

Leonarda. Not now, but later on. There will come a time—

Hagbart. Yes, a time of work—of self-development! It has come now. That is why I am here! Perhaps a time of conflict may come too—heaven send that it may! Are we to pay any heed to that? No! You are free, and I am free; and our future is in our own hands.

Leonarda. Besides, I have grown old—

Hagbart. You!

Leonarda. —and jealous, and troublesome; while you are the incarnation of youth and joy.

Hagbart. You have more youth in you than I. You are an enchantress! All your life you will be showing me new aspects of yourself—as you are doing now. Each year will invest you with a new beauty, new spiritual power. Do you think I only half understand you, or only half love you? I want to sit close in your heart, warmed by its glow. It is the irresistible power of truth that has drawn me to you. My whole life will not be long enough for me to sound the unfathomable depths of your soul.

Leonarda. Your words are like the spring breezes, alluring and intoxicating, but full of deadly peril too.

Hagbart. You love me! I knew it before I came here to-day. I saw it the moment I stood here. Love is the very breath of life to you, surpassingly more than to any one else I have ever seen; and that is why you have suffered so terribly from the disappointments and emptiness of life. And now, when love is calling to you—love that is true and sincere—you are trembling!

Leonarda. You understand me in a way I thought impossible! It takes away all my resolution; it—

Hagbart. Surely you saw it in all the many talks we have had?

Leonarda. Yes.

Hagbart. Then is that not a proof that we two—?

Leonarda. Yes, it is true! I can hide nothing from you. (*Bursts into tears.*)

Hagbart. But why this unhappiness?

Leonarda. I don't know! It pursues me all day, and all through the sleepless night. (*Weeps helplessly.*)

Hagbart. But it has no real existence. It might, in the case of others; but not in our case—not for us.

Leonarda. I spoke in my distress, without thinking. I threw out the first thing that came into my head, to try and stop you. But it is not that—oh, God! (*Sways as if half swooning.*)

Hagbart (*rushing to her side*). Leonarda!

Leonarda. No, no! Let me be!

Hagbart. You know your love is too strong for you—will you not give way to it?

Leonarda. Hagbart, there is something about it that is not right—

Hagbart. Do you mean in the way it has come about? In Aagot's having been the means of leading me to you? Think of it, and you will see that it could not have happened otherwise.

Leonarda. Talking about it will not help me. I must see Aagot; I must speak to Aagot.

Hagbart. But you have done that! You know it is you that love me, and not she. You know it is you that I love, and not her. What more do you need?

Leonarda. I want time. I want not to lose the self-control I have won for myself by years of renunciation and self-sacrifice, and was so proud of. But it won't obey me when you speak to me. Your words possess me in spite of myself. If there is any happiness on earth, it is to find one's every thought faultlessly understood. But that happiness brings a pain with it—for me, at any rate. No, don't answer! You are too strong for me; because I love you—love you as only one can who has never believed such joy could exist or could possibly come to her—and now the depths of my peace are troubled with the thought that it is treachery to my child.

Hagbart. But you know that it is not!

Leonarda. I don't know. Let me have time to think! I am afraid, and my fear revives forgotten memories. More than that—I am afraid of the immensity of my love for you, afraid of dragging you with me into a whirlpool of disaster!—No, don't answer! Don't touch me!— Hagbart, do you love me?

Hagbart. Can you ask that?

Leonarda. Then help me! Go away!—Be generous. Let my heart know this triumph and see you in its glorious rays! Other women do not need that, perhaps— but I need it—go!

Hagbart. Leonarda!

Leonarda. Wait till you hear from me. It will not be long. Whatever happens, be patient—and remember, I love you!—No, don't say anything! I have neither courage nor strength for anything more. (*Her voice sinks to a whisper.*) Go! (*He turns to go.*) Hagbart! (*He stops.*) What you have said to me to-day has given me the greatest happiness of my life. But your going away now without a word will be more to me than all you have said. (*He goes out.*)

Leonarda (*stands for some moments in a kind of ecstasy, moves, and stands still again. Suddenly she calls out*): Aagot!

Aagot (*from without*). Are you there?

Leonarda. My dear child! (*Goes out, and comes in again with* AAGOT *in her arms.*)   Did you walk?

Aagot. The whole way! (*She is carrying her hat in her hand, appears hot and sunburnt, and bears evident signs of having made a long journey on foot. She takes off a knapsack which she has been carrying on her back.*)   I washed in a brook to-day and used it as a looking-glass as well!

Leonarda. Have you been walking all night?

Aagot. No; I slept for a little while at Opsal, but I was out by sunrise.   It was lovely!

Leonarda. And I have just been arranging to send and fetch you.

Aagot. Really?   Well, they can fetch my things.   I could not wait any longer.

Leonarda. You look so well.

Aagot. Oh, that is because I am so sunburnt.

Leonarda. You are feeling all right again, then—now?

Aagot. Splendid, aunt!   All that is over, now.—I have had a letter from grandmother.

Leonarda. Was that letter from her that I sent on to you?   I could not make out whom it was from.

Aagot. Yes, it was from her.   Here it is.   You must hear it.

Leonarda. Yes.

Aagot (*reads*). " My dear child.   I have not written a letter for many years, so I do not know what this will be like.   But Hagbart is away, so I must tell you myself. Do not be distressed any longer.   As soon as you are married, I will come and live with you."   Isn't that glorious, aunt? (*She is trembling with happiness, and throws her arms round* LEONARDA'S *neck.*)

Leonarda. But—

Aagot. But what?   There is no more " but " about it, don't you see!   It is on your account.

Leonarda. On my account? Yes, but — what about you? How do you stand—with Hagbart?

Aagot. Oh, that?—Well, I will tell you the whole story! I can do that now.—Oh, don't take it all so seriously, aunt! It really is nothing. But let us sit down. (*Brings forward a seat, as she speaks.*) I really feel as if I wanted to sit down for a little while, too!—Well, you see, it came upon me like an unexpected attack—a blow from behind, as it were. Now, my dear aunt, don't look so troubled. It is all over now. As a matter of fact, the beginning of it all was a play I saw.

Leonarda. A play?

Aagot. We saw it together once, you and I. do you remember? Scribe's *Bataille de Dames*.

Leonarda. Yes.

Aagot. And I remember thinking and saying to you: That fellow Henri, in the play, was a stupid fellow. He had the choice between a strong-natured, handsome, spirited woman, who was ready to give her life for him, and a child who was really a stupid little thing—for she was, it is no use denying it, aunt—and he chose the insignificant little person. No, I would rather sit down here; I can rest better so. Ah, that is good! And now you mustn't look me in the face oftener than I want to let you, because you take it too dreadfully solemnly, and I am going to tell you something foolish now.—All of a sudden it flashed across my mind: Good heavens! the woman was ——, and the little hussy with the curly hair was ——, and he? But Hagbart is a man of some sense; he had chosen otherwise! And I did not know; but I realised at the same time that almost from the first day Hagbart used always to talk to you, and only to you, and hardly at all to me except to talk about you. I got so miserable about it that I felt as if some one had put a knife into my heart; and from that moment—I am so ashamed of it now—I had no more peace. I carried an aching pain in my heart night and day, and I thought my heart itself would break merely to see him speak to you or you to him. I am ashamed of myself; because what was more natural than that he should never be tired of talking to you? I never should, myself!

Leonarda. But still I don't see—I don't understand yet—

Aagot. Wait a bit! Oh, don't look so anxiously at me! It is all over now, you know.

Leonarda. What is all over?

Aagot. Bless my soul, wait! Aunt, dear, you are more impatient than I am myself! I do not want you to think me worse than I am, so I must first tell you how I fought with myself. I lay and cried all night, because I could not talk to you about it, and in the daytime I forced myself to seem merry and lively and happy. And then, aunt, one day I said to myself quite honestly: Why should you feel aggrieved at his loving her more than you? What are you, compared with her? And how splendid it would be, I thought, for my dear aunt to find some one she could truly love, and that it should be I that had brought them together!

Leonarda. That was splendid of you, Aagot!

Aagot. Yes, but now I mustn't make myself out better than I am, either. Because I did not always manage to look at it that way; very often something very like a sob kept rising in my throat. But then I used to talk to myself seriously, and say: Even supposing it is your own happiness you are giving up for her sake, is that too much for you to do for her? No, a thousand times no! And even supposing he does not love you any more, ought you not to be able to conquer your own feelings? Surely it

G

would be cowardly not to be able to do that! Think no more of him, if he does not love you!

Leonarda. Aagot, I cannot tell you how I admire you, and love you, and how proud I am of you!

Aagot. Oh, aunt, I never realised as I did then what you have been to me! I knew that if I were capable of any great deed, anything really good or really fine, it was you that had planted the impulse in me. And then I sought every opportunity to bring this about; I wanted to take ever so humble a part in it, but without your hearing a word or a sigh from me. Besides, I had you always before me as an example; because I knew that you would have done it for me—indeed that you had already done as much. Your example was like a shining beacon to me, aunt!

Leonarda. Aagot!

Aagot. But you don't seem to be as happy about it as I am! Don't you understand yet how it all happened?

Leonarda. Yes, but—about the result of it?

Aagot. Dearest, you know all about that!—No, it is true, you don't! I must not forget to tell you that; otherwise you won't be able to understand why I behaved so stupidly at the Bishop's.

Leonarda. No.

Aagot. Well, you see, when I was full of this splendid determination to sacrifice myself so as to make you happy, I used to feel a regular fury come over me because Hagbart noticed no change in me—or, to be more correct, did not understand it in the least. He used to go about as if he were in a dream. Isn't it extraordinary how one thing leads to another? My feeling was stronger than I had any idea of; because when the Bishop wanted to slight you—and that was like a stab from behind, too!—I absolutely lost my head with Hagbart because of his not having prevented that, instead of going about dreaming. I don't know—but—well, you saw yourself what happened. I blurted out the first thing that came into my head and was abominably rude; you were angry; then we made friends again and I went away—and then, aunt—

Leonarda. And then—?

Aagot. Then I thought it all over! All the beautiful things you said to me about him, as we were going home, came back to me more and more forcibly. I saw you as I had always known you, noble and gentle.—It was so wonderful up there, too! The air, the clearness, the sense of space! And the lake, almost always calm, because it was so sheltered! And the wonderful stillness, especially in the evening!—And so it healed, just as a wound heals.

Leonarda. What healed?

Aagot. The pain in my heart, aunt. All the difficulties vanished. I know Hagbart to be what you said—noble and true. And you too, aunt! You would neither of you have wished to give me a moment's pain, even unconsciously, I knew. It was so good to realise that! It was so restful, that often while I was thinking of it, I went to sleep where I sat—I was so happy!—Ah, how I love him! And then came grandmother's letter—.

HANS *comes in, but does not see* AAGOT *at first.*

Hans. Then I am to fetch Miss Aagot—why, there she is!

Aagot (*getting up*). You quite frightened me, Hans!

Hans. Welcome back, miss!

Aagot. Thank you.

Hans. Well, you have saved me a journey, miss, I suppose?

Aagot. Yes. But some one must go and fetch my things.

Hans. Of course, miss.—But what is the matter with the mistress?

Aagot. Aunt!—Heavens, what is the matter?

Hans. The mistress has not looked well lately.

Aagot. Hasn't she? Aunt, dear! Shall I—? Would you like to—? Aunt!

Hans. Shall I fetch some one to—

Leonarda. No, no!—But you, Aagot—will you—. Oh, my God!—Will you run in—and get—

Aagot. Your bottle of drops?

Leonarda. Yes. (AAGOT *runs out.*) Hans, go as quickly as you can to the General's—ask him to come here! At once!

Hans. Yes, ma'am.

Leonarda. Hans!

Hans. Yes, ma'am.

Leonarda. Go on horseback. You may not find the General at home—and have to go elsewhere after him.

Hans. Yes, ma'am. (*Goes out.* AAGOT *re-enters.*)

Aagot. Here it is, aunt!

Leonarda. Thank you. It is over now.

Aagot. But what was it, aunt?

Leonarda. It was something, dear — something that comes over one sometimes at the change of the year.

Curtain.

(*The interval between this act and the next should be very short.*)

ACT IV

(SCENE.—*A room in the* BISHOP'S *house, the same evening. The lights are lit. The* BISHOP *comes in with* LEONARDA, *who is in travelling dress, with a shawl over her arm and a bag in her hand. The* BISHOP *makes a movement as though to relieve her of them, but she puts them down herself.*)

Leonarda. Your lordship must excuse me for troubling you so late as this; but the reason of it is something over which I have no control.—Is your nephew here?

Bishop. No, but I expect him. He has been here twice this afternoon already to see me, but I was out.

Leonarda. I will make haste then, and do what I have to do before he comes.

Bishop. Shall I give instructions that we are to be told when he comes in?

Leonarda. If you please.

Bishop (*ringing the bell*). Grandmother says that as soon as he came back to-day, he went at once to see you.

Leonarda. Yes.

Enter a Maid.

Bishop (*to the* Maid). Be so good as to let me know when Mr. Hagbart comes in. (*Exit* Maid.)

Leonarda. Has he had a talk with his grandmother?

Bishop. Yes.

Leonarda. After he—? (*Checks herself.*)

Bishop. After he had been to see you.

Leonarda. Did he tell her anything?

Bishop. He was very much agitated, apparently. I did not ask grandmother any further questions; I can imagine what passed between them.—Has he spoken to you?

Leonarda. Yes.

Bishop. And you, Mrs. Falk?

Leonarda. I—? Well, I am here.

Bishop. Going on a journey, if I am not mistaken?

Leonarda. Going on a journey. Things are turning out as you wished after all, my lord.

Bishop. And he is to know nothing about it?

Leonarda. No one—except the person who will accompany me. I am sailing for England by to-night's boat.

Bishop (*looking at his watch*). You haven't much time, then.

Leonarda. I only want to entrust to your lordship a deed of gift of my property here.

Bishop. In favour of your niece?

Leonarda. Yes, for Aagot. She shall have everything.

Bishop. But last time, Mrs. Falk, you said—

Leonarda. Oh, I have enough for my journey. Later on I shall want nothing; I can provide for myself.

Bishop. But what about Aagot? Will you not wait until she comes home?

Leonarda. She came home to-day. She is resting now. But I have sent back my carriage to bring her here immediately. I want to ask you to take her in — I know no one else—and to comfort her—

Bishop. Indeed I will, Mrs. Falk. I understand what this must cost you.

Leonarda. And will you try—to—to bring those two together again?

Bishop. But they don't love each other!

Leonarda. Aagot loves him. And—as they both love me—my idea was that when I am gone, and they know that it was my wish, the love they both have for me may bring them together again. I hope so—they are both so young.

Bishop. I will do all I can.

Leonarda. Thank you. And I want to make bold to beg you to let grandmother go and live in the country with Aagot—or let Aagot come and live here, whichever they prefer. It would divert Aagot's mind if she had the care of grandmother; and she is very fond of her.

Bishop. And grandmother of her.

Leonarda. And wherever the grandmother is, Hagbart will be too. Very likely the old lady would help them.

Bishop. I think your idea is an excellent one; and I am amazed that you have had time and strength to think it all out in this manner.

Leonarda. Is grandmother still up?

Bishop. Yes; I have just come from her room. Hagbart has excited her; she can stand so little.

Leonarda. Then I expect I had better not go and bid her good-bye. I should have liked to, otherwise.

Bishop. I don't think I ought to allow it.

Leonarda. Then please say good-bye to her from me— and thank her.

Bishop. I will.

Leonarda. And ask her—to help—

Bishop. I will do everything I possibly can.

Leonarda. And your lordship must forgive me for all the upset I have caused here. I did not intend it.

Bishop. I am only sorry that I did not know you sooner. Many things might have been different.

Leonarda. We won't talk about that now.

Enter Maid.

Maid. I was asked to bring you this card, ma'am.

Leonarda. Thank you. Is the General in the hall?

Maid. Yes.

Bishop. General Rosen—here?

Leonarda. I took the liberty of asking him to call for me here when the boat was signalled.

Bishop. Ask the General to come in. (*Exit* Maid.) Then it is General Rosen that is to—. (*Checks himself.*)

Leonarda (*searching in her bag*). —that is to accompany me? He is my husband.

Bishop. The husband you divorced.

Leonarda. Yes.

Bishop. I see I have done you a great injustice, Mrs. Falk.

Leonarda. Yes. (GENERAL ROSEN *comes in, dressed in a smart travelling suit and looking very spruce.*)

General Rosen. I beg your lordship's pardon — but, time is up.—Mrs. Falk, is this yours? (*Gives her a letter.*)

Leonarda. Yes.—When Aagot comes, will your lordship give her this?—and help her?

Bishop. I will, Mrs. Falk. God bless you!

Enter Maid.

Maid. Mr. Hagbart has just come in.

Leonarda. Good-bye!—Say good-bye to—

Bishop (*taking her hand*). What you are doing is more than any one of us could have done.

Leonarda. It all depends on how deeply one loves.—
Thank you, and good-bye!

Bishop. Good-bye! (GENERAL ROSEN *offers* LEONARDA
his arm. She takes it, and they go out. The BISHOP *follows
them.* HAGBART *comes in from the right, looks round in
astonishment, then goes towards the back of the room and
meets the* BISHOP *in the doorway.*)

Bishop. Is that you? (*Both come forward without
speaking.*)

Hagbart (*in a low voice, but evidently under the influence
of great emotion*). I can tell by your voice—and your face
—that you know about it.

Bishop. You mean that you think I have had a talk
with grandmother?

Hagbart. Yes.

Bishop. Well, I have. She told me nothing definite,
but I see how things stand. I saw that sooner than you
did yourself, you know.

Hagbart. That is true. The fight is over now, as far as
I am concerned.

Bishop. Scarcely that, Hagbart.

Hagbart. Oh, you won't admit it, I know. But I call it
the most decisive victory of my life. I love Mrs. Falk—
and she loves me.

Bishop. If you were not in such an excited con-
dition—

Hagbart. It is not excitement, it is happiness. But
here, with you—oh, I have not come to ask for your
blessing; we must do without that! But I have come to
tell you the fact, because it was my duty to do so.—Does
it grieve you so much?

Bishop. Yes.

Hagbart. Uncle, I feel hurt at that.

Bishop. My boy—!

Hagbart. I feel hurt both on her account and on my own. It shows that you know neither of us.

Bishop. Let us sit down and talk quietly, Hagbart.

Hagbart. I must ask you to make no attempt to persuade me to alter my decision.

Bishop. Make your mind easy on that score. Your feelings do you honour—and I know now that she is worthy of them.

Hagbart. What—do you say that? (*They sit down.*)

Bishop. My dear Hagbart, let me tell you this at once. I have gone through an experience, too, since the last time we met. And it has taught me that I had no right to treat Mrs. Falk as I did.

Hagbart. Is it possible?

Bishop. I judged her both too quickly and too harshly. That is one of our besetting sins. And I have paid too much heed to the opinion of others, and too little to the charity that should give us courage to do good. She, whom I despised, has taught me that.

Hagbart. You do not know how grateful and how happy you have made me by saying that!

Bishop. I have something more to say. At the time we held that unjust opinion of her, we misled you—for you relied on our opinion then—until you ended by sharing our views and being even more vehement in the matter than we, as young people will. That created a reaction in you, which in the end led to love. If that love had been a sin, we should have been to blame for it.

Hagbart. Is it a sin, then?

Bishop. No. But when you felt that we were inclined to look upon it in that light, that very fact stirred up your sense of justice and increased your love. You have a noble heart.

Hagbart. Ah, how I shall love you after this, uncle!

Bishop. And that is why I wanted you to sit down here just now, Hagbart—to beg your pardon—and hers. And my congregation's, too. It is my duty to guide them, but I was not willing to trust them enough. By far the greater number among them are good people; they would have followed me if I had had the courage to go forward.

Hagbart. Uncle, I admire and revere you more than I have ever done before—more than any one has ever done!

Bishop (getting up). My dear boy!

Hagbart (throwing himself into his arms). Uncle!

Bishop. Is your love strong enough to bear—

Hagbart. Anything!

Bishop. Because sometimes love is given to us to teach us self-sacrifice.

The GRANDMOTHER *comes in.*

Grandmother. I heard Hagbart's voice.

Hagbart. Grandmother! (*He and the* BISHOP *go to help her.*) Grandmother! You don't know how happy I am! (*Takes her by the arm.*)

Grandmother. Is that true?

Bishop (taking her other arm). You should not walk about without help.

Grandmother. I heard Hagbart's voice. He was talking so loud, that I thought something had happened.

Hagbart. So it has—something good! Uncle consents! He is splendid! He has made everything all right again, and better than ever! Oh, grandmother, I wish you were not so old! I feel as if I should like to take you up in my arms and dance you round the room.

Grandmother. You mustn't do that, my dear. (*They put her into her chair.*) Now! What is your last bit of news?

Hagbart. My last bit of news? I have no fresh news! There is nothing more to tell!

Bishop. Yes, Hagbart, there is.

Hagbart. Why do you say that so seriously?—You look so serious—and seem agitated! Uncle! (*The noise of wheels is heard outside.*)

Bishop. Wait a little, my dear boy. Wait a little! (*Goes out by the door at the back.*)

Hagbart. Grandmother, what can it be?

Grandmother. I don't know.—But happiness is often so brief.

Hagbart. Happiness so brief? What do you mean?— Good God, grandmother, don't torture me!

Grandmother. I assure you, I know nothing about it— only—

Hagbart. Only—what?

Grandmother. While your uncle was with me, Mrs. Falk was announced.

Hagbart. Mrs. Falk? Has she been here? Just now?

Grandmother. Yes, just now.

Hagbart. Then something must have happened! Perhaps it was she that uncle—. (*Rushes to the door, which opens, and the* BISHOP *comes in with* AAGOT *on his arm, followed by* CORNELIA.) Aagot!

Aagot. Hagbart!— (*Anxiously.*) Is aunt not here!

Cornelia. What, grandmother here! (*Goes to her.*)

Bishop. My dear Aagot, your aunt entrusted this letter to me to give to you.

Hagbart. A letter—?

Grandmother. What is the matter? Let me see! (*CORNELIA moves her chair nearer to the others.*)

Hagbart. Read it aloud, Aagot!

Aagot (*reads*). "My darling. When you receive this

letter I shall have—gone away.　I love the man you—."
(*With a cry, she falls swooning.　The* BISHOP *catches her
in his arms.*)

Grandmother. She has gone away?

Cornelia. She loves the man you—?　Good God, look
at Hagbart!

Bishop. Cornelia!　(*She goes to him, and they lay* AAGOT
on the couch. CORNELIA *stays beside her.　The* BISHOP
turns to HAGBART.)　Hagbart!　(HAGBART *throws himself
into his arms.*)　Courage!　Courage, my boy!

Grandmother (*getting up*). It is like going back to the
days of great emotions!

The Curtain falls slowly.

A GAUNTLET

A PLAY IN THREE ACTS

DRAMATIS PERSONÆ

Riis.
Mrs. Riis.
Svava, their daughter.
Margit, their maid.
Christensen.
Mrs. Christensen.
Alfred, their son, betrothed to Svava.
Dr. Nordan.
Thomas, his servant.
Hoff.

The action of the play passes in Christiania.

A GAUNTLET

ACT I

(SCENE.—*A room in* RIIS' *house. An open door at the back leads into a park and gives a glimpse of the sea beyond. Windows on each side of the door. Doors also in the right and left walls. Beyond the door on the right is a piano ; opposite to the piano a cupboard. In the foreground, to the right and left, two couches with small tables in front of them. Easy-chairs and smaller chairs scattered about.* MRS. RIIS *is sitting on the couch to the left, and* DR. NORDAN *in a chair in the centre of the room. He is wearing a straw hat pushed on to the back of his head, and has a large handkerchief spread over his knees. He is sitting with his arms folded, leaning upon his stick.*)

Mrs. Riis. A penny for your thoughts!

Nordan. What was it you were asking me about?

Mrs. Riis. About that matter of Mrs. North, of course.

Nordan. That matter of Mrs. North? Well, I was talking to Christensen about it just now. He has advanced the money and is going to try and get the bank to suspend proceedings. I have told you that already. What else do you want to know?

Mrs. Riis. I want to know how much gossip there is about it, my dear friend.

Nordan. Oh, men don't gossip about each other's affairs. —By the way, isn't our friend in there (*nodding towards the door on the right*) going to be told about it? This seems a good opportunity.

Mrs. Riis. Let us wait.

Nordan. Because Christensen will have to be repaid, you know. I told him he would be.

Mrs. Riis. Naturally. What else would you suppose?

Nordan (*getting up*). Well, I am going away for my holidays, so Christensen must look after it now.—Was it a very grand party yesterday?

Mrs. Riis. There was not much display.

Nordan. No, the Christensens' parties are never very luxurious. But I suppose there were a lot of people?

Mrs. Riis. I have never seen so many at a private entertainment.

Nordan. Is Svava up?

Mrs. Riis. She is out bathing.

Nordan. Already? Did you come home early, then?

Mrs. Riis. At about twelve, I think. Svava wanted to come home. My husband was late, I think.

Nordan. The card tables. She looked radiant, I suppose, eh?

Mrs. Riis. Why didn't you come?

Nordan. I never go to betrothal parties, and I never go to weddings—never! I can't bear the sight of the poor victims in their veils and wreaths.

Mrs. Riis. But, my dear doctor, you surely think—as we all do—that this will be a happy marriage?

Nordan. He is a fine lad. But, all the same—I have been taken in so often.—Oh, well!

Mrs. Riis. She was so happy, and is just as happy to-day.

Nordan. It is a pity I shall not see her. Good-bye, Mrs. Riis.

Mrs. Riis. Good-bye, doctor. Then you are off to-day?

Nordan. Yes, I need a change of air.

Mrs. Riis. Quite so. Well, I hope you will enjoy yourself—and, many thanks for what you have done!

Nordan. It is I ought to thank you, my dear lady! I am vexed not to be able to say good-bye to Svava. (*Goes out.* MRS. RIIS *takes up a magazine from the table on the left and settles herself comfortably on a couch from which she can see into the park. During what follows she reads whenever opportunity allows.* RIIS *comes in through the door on the right, in his shirt sleeves and struggling with his collar.*)

Riis. Good morning! Was that Nordan that went out just now?

Mrs. Riis. Yes. (RIIS *crosses the room, then turns back and disappears through the door on the right. He comes back again immediately and goes through the same proceeding, all the time busy with his collar.*) Can I help you at all?

Riis. No—thanks all the same! These new-fangled shirts are troublesome things. I bought some in Paris.

Mrs. Riis. Yes, I believe you have bought a whole dozen.

Riis. A dozen and a half. (*Goes into his room, comes out again in apparently the same difficulties, and walks about as before.*) As a matter of fact I am wondering about something.

Mrs. Riis. It must be something complicated.

Riis. It is—it is. No doubt of it!—This collar is the very— Ah, at last! (*Goes into his room and comes out again, this time with his necktie in his hand.*) I have been wondering—wondering—what our dear girl's character is made up of?

Mrs. Riis. What it is made up of?

Riis. Yes—what characteristics she gets from you and

what from me, and so forth. In what respects, that is to say, she takes after your family, and in what respects after mine, and so forth. Svava is a remarkable girl.

Mrs. Riis. She is that.

Riis. She is neither altogether you nor altogether me; nor is she exactly a compound of us both.

Mrs. Riis. Svava is something more than that.

Riis. A considerable deal more than that, too. (*Disappears again; then comes out with his coat on, brushing himself.*) What did you say?

Mrs. Riis. I did not speak.—I rather think it is my mother that Svava is most like.

Riis. I should think so! Svava, with her quiet, pleasant ways! What a thing to say!

Mrs. Riis. Svava can be passionate enough.

Riis. Svava never forgets her manners as your mother did.

Mrs. Riis. You never understood mother. Still, no doubt they are unlike in a great many things.

Riis. Absolutely!—Can you see now how right I was in chattering to her in various languages from the beginning, even when she was quite tiny? Can you see that now? You were opposed to my doing it.

Mrs. Riis. I was opposed to your perpetually plaguing the child, and also to the endless jumping from one thing to another.

Riis. But look at the result, my dear! Look at the result! (*Begins to hum a tune.*)

Mrs. Riis. You are surely never going to pretend that it is the languages that have made her what she is?

Riis (*as he disappears*). No, not the languages; but— (*His voice is heard from within his room*)—the languages have done a wonderful lot! She has *savoir vivre*—what? (*Comes out again.*)

Mrs. Riis. I am sure that is not what Svava is most admired for.

Riis. No, no. On the boat, a man asked me if I were related to the Miss Riis who had founded the Kindergartens in the town. I said I had the honour to be her father. You should have seen his face! I nearly had a fit.

Mrs. Riis. Yes, the Kindergartens have been a great success from the very first.

Riis. And they are responsible for her getting engaged, too—aren't they? What?

Mrs. Riis. You must ask her.

Riis. You have never even noticed my new suit.

Mrs. Riis. Indeed I have.

Riis. I didn't hear as much as the tiniest cry of admiration from you. Look at the harmony of it all!—the scheme of colour, even down to the shoes!—what? And the handkerchief, too!

Mrs. Riis. How old are you, dear?

Riis. Hold your tongue!—Anyway, how old do you think people take me to be?

Mrs. Riis. Forty, of course.

Riis. " Of course "? I don't see that it is so obvious.— This suit is a kind of Bridal Symphony, composed at Cologne when I got the telegram telling me of Svava's engagement. Just think of it! At Cologne—not ten hours' journey from Paris! But I could not wait ten hours; I had risen too much in my own estimation in view of my approaching relationship with the richest family in the country.

Mrs. Riis. Is that suit all you have to show for it, then?

Riis. What a question! Just you wait till I have got my luggage through the custom-house!

Mrs. Riis. We shall be quite out of it, I suppose?

Riis. You out of it! When a very lucky daddy finds himself in Paris at a most tremendous moment—

Mrs. Riis. And what did you think of the party yesterday?

Riis. I was quite delighted with the boat for being late, so that I was landed in the middle of a *fête champêtre* as if by magic. And naturally one had a tremendous welcome, as the party was in honour of one's own only daughter!

Mrs. Riis. What time did you come in last night?

Riis. Don't you understand that we had to play cards yesterday, too? I could not get out of it; I had to make a fourth with Abraham, Isaac, and Jacob—that is to say, with our host, a cabinet minister, and old Holk. It was a tremendous honour to lose one's money to grand folk like that. Because I always lose, you know.—I came home about three o'clock, I should think.—What is that you are reading?

Mrs. Riis. The *Fortnightly.*

Riis. Has there been anything good in it while I have been away? (*Begins to hum a tune.*)

Mrs. Riis. Yes—there is an article here on heredity that you must read. It has some reference to what we began to talk about.

Riis. Do you know this tune? (*Goes over to the piano.*) It is all the rage now. I heard it all over Germany. (*Begins to play and sing, but breaks off suddenly.*) I will go and fetch the music, while I think of it! (*Goes into his room and comes out again with the music. Sits down and begins to play and sing again.* SVAVA *comes in by the door on the left.* RIIS *stops when he sees her, and jumps up.*) Good morning, my child! Good morning! I have hardly had a chance to say a word to you yet. At the party every one took you away from me! (*Kisses her, and comes forward with her.*)

Svava. Why were you so long of coming back from abroad?

Riis. Why don't people give one some warning when they are going to get engaged?

Svava. Because people don't know anything about it themselves, till it happens! Good morning again, mother. (*Kneels down beside her.*)

Mrs. Riis. There is a delicious freshness about you, dear! Did you have a walk in the wood after your swim?

Svava (*getting up*). Yes, and just as I got home a few minutes ago Alfred passed the house and called up to me. He is coming in directly.

Riis. To tell you the truth—and one ought always to tell the truth—I had quite given up the hope of such happiness coming to our dear girl.

Svava. I know you had. I had quite given it up myself.

Riis. Until your fairy prince came?

Svava. Until my fairy prince came. And he took his time about it, too!

Riis. You had been waiting for him a long time, though —hadn't you?

Svava. Not a bit of it! I never once thought of him.

Riis. Now you are talking in riddles.

Svava. Yes, it is a riddle to understand how two people, who have seen each other from childhood without even giving each other a thought, suddenly—! Because that was really how it happened. It all dates from a certain moment—and then, all at once, he became quite another man in my eyes.

Riis. But in every one else's, I suppose, he is the same as before?

Svava. I hope so!

Riis. He is more lively than he was, at any rate—in my eyes.

Svava. Yes, I saw you laughing together last night. What was it?

Riis. We were discussing the best way of getting through the world. I gave him my three famous rules of life.

Mrs. Riis and Svava (together). Already!

Riis. They were a great success. Do you remember them, you bad girl?

Svava. Rule number one: Never make a fool of yourself.

Riis. Rule number two: Never be a burden to any one.

Svava. Rule number three: Always be in the fashion. They are not very hard to remember, because they are neither obscure nor profound.

Riis. But all the harder to put into practice! And that is a great virtue in all rules of life.—I congratulate you on your new morning frock. Under the circumstances it is really charming.

Svava. " Under the circumstances " means, I suppose, considering that you have had no hand in it.

Riis. Yes, because I should never have chosen that trimming. However, the " under the circumstances " is not so bad. A good cut, too—yes. Aha! just you wait till my portmanteau comes!

Svava. Some surprises for us?

Riis. Big ones!—By the way, I have something here. *(Goes into his room.)*

Svava. Do you know, mother, he seems to me more restless than ever.

Mrs. Riis. That is happiness, dear.

Svava. And yet father's restlessness has always something a little sad about it. He is—. (RIIS *comes out of his room again.*) Do you know what I heard a cabinet minister say about you yesterday?

Riis. A man of that stamp is sure to say something worth hearing.

Svava. " We all always look upon your father, Miss Riis, as our well-dressed man *par excellence.*"

Riis. Ah, *a bien dit son excellence !* But I can tell you something better than that.   You are getting your father a knighthood.

Svava. I am?

Riis. Yes, who else?   Of course the Government has once or twice made use of me to some small degree in connection with various commercial treaties; but now, as our great man's brother-in-law, I am going to be made a Knight of St. Olaf!

Svava. I congratulate you.

Riis. Well, when it rains on the parson it drips on the clerk, you know.

Svava. You are really most unexpectedly modest in your new position.

Riis. Am I not!—And now you shall see me as a modest showman of beautiful dresses—that is to say, of drawings of dresses—still more modest than the showman, from the latest play at the Français.

Svava. Oh no, dad—not now!

Mrs. Riis. We won't start on that till the afternoon.

Riis. One would really think I were the only woman of the lot!   However, as you please.   You rule the world! Well, then, I have another proposition to make, in two parts.   Part one, that we sit down!

Svava. We sit down! (*She and her father sit.*)

Riis. And next, that you tell your newly-returned parent exactly how it all happened.   All about that " riddle," you know!

Svava. Oh, that!—You must excuse me; I cannot tell you about that.

Riis. Not in all its sweet details, of course! Good heavens, who would be so barbarous as to ask such a thing in the first delicious month of an engagement! No, I only want you to tell us what was the *primum mobile* in the matter.

Svava. Oh, I understand. Yes, I will tell you that, because that really means teaching you to know Alfred's true character.

Riis. For instance—how did you come to speak to him?

Svava. Well, that was those darling Kindergartens of ours—

Riis. Oho!—*Your* darling Kindergartens, you mean?

Svava. What, when there are over a hundred girls there—?

Riis. Never mind about that! I suppose he came to bring a donation?

Svava. Yes, he came several times with a donation—

Riis. Aha!

Svava. And one day we were talking about luxury— saying that it was better to use one's time and money in our way, than to use them in luxurious living.

Riis. But how do you define luxury?

Svava. We did not discuss that at all. But I saw that he considered luxury to be immoral.

Riis. Luxury immoral!

Svava. Yes, I know that is not your opinion. But it is mine.

Riis. Your mother's, you mean, and your grand-mother's.

Svava. Exactly; but mine too, if you don't object?

Riis. Not I!

Svava. I mentioned that little incident that happened to us when we were in America—do you remember? We had gone to a temperance meeting, and saw women drive up who were going to support the cause of abstinence, and yet were—well, of course we did not know their circumstances—but to judge from their appearance, with their carriages and horses, their jewellery and dresses—especially their jewellery—they must have been worth, say—

Riis. Say many thousands of dollars! No doubt about it.

Svava. There *is* no doubt about it. And don't you think that is really just as disgraceful debauchery, in its own way, as drink is in its?

Riis. Oh, well—!

Svava. Yes, you shrug your shoulders. Alfred did not do that. He told me of his own experiences—in great cities. It was horrible!

Riis. What was horrible?

Svava. The contrast between poverty and wealth—between the bitterest want and the most reckless luxury.

Riis. Oh — that! I thought, perhaps—. However, go on!

Svava. He did not sit looking quite indifferent and clean his nails.

Riis. I beg your pardon.

Svava. Oh, please go on, dear!—No, he prophesied a great social revolution, and spoke so fervently about it—and it was then that he told me what his ideas about wealth were. It was the greatest possible surprise to me—and a new idea to me, too, to some extent. You should have seen how handsome he looked!

Riis. Handsome, did you say?

Svava. Isn't he handsome? I think so, at all events. And so does mother, I think?

Mrs. Riis (without looking up from her book). And so does mother.

Riis. Mothers always fall in love with their daughters' young men—but they fall out again when they become their mothers-in-law!

Svava. Is that your experience?

Riis. That is my experience. So Alfred Christensen has blossomed into a beauty? Well, we must consider that settled.

Svava. He stood there so sure of himself, and looking so honest and clean—for that is an essential thing, you know.

Riis. What exactly do you mean by " clean," my dear?

Svava. I mean just what the word means.

Riis. Exactly—but I want to know what meaning you attach to the word.

Svava. Well—the meaning that I hope any one would attach to it if they used the word of me.

Riis. Do you attach the same meaning to it if it is used of a man, as you would if it were used of a girl?

Svava. Yes, of course.

Riis. And do you suppose that Christensen's son—

Svava (getting up). Father, you are insulting me!

Riis. How can the fact of his being his father's son be an insult to you?

Svava. In that respect he is not his father's son! I am not likely to make any mistake in a thing of that sort!

Mrs. Riis. I am just reading about inherited tendencies. It is not necessary to suppose that he has inherited all of his father's.

Riis. Oh, well—have it as you please! I am afraid of all these superhuman theories of yours. You will never get through the world with them.

Svava. What do you mean?—Mother, what does father mean?

Mrs. Riis. I suppose he means that all men are alike. And one must allow that it is true.

Svava. You do not really mean that?

Riis. But why get so excited about it?—Come and sit down! And, besides, how can you possibly tell?

Svava. Tell? What?

Riis. Well, in each individual case—

Svava. —whether the man I see standing before me or walking past me is an unclean, disgusting beast—or a man?

Riis. Etcetera, etcetera!—You may make mistakes, my dear Svava?

Svava. No—not any more than I should make a mistake about you, father, when you begin to tease me with your horrid principles! Because, in spite of them, you are the chastest and most refined man I know.

Mrs. Riis (laying down her book). Are you going to keep that morning frock on, dear child? Won't you change your dress before Alfred comes?

Svava. No, mother, I am not going to be put off like that.—By this time I have seen so many of my girl friends giving themselves trustfully to their " fairy prince," as they think, and waking in the arms of a beast. I shall not risk that! I shall not make that mistake!

Mrs. Riis. Well, as it is, there is no occasion for you to get heated about it. Alfred is a man of honour.

Svava. He is. But I have heard of one shocking experience after another. There was poor Helga, only a month ago! And I myself—I can speak about it now, for I am happy now and feel secure—I can tell you now why I have been so long about it. For a long time I did not dare to trust myself; because I too have been on the brink of being deceived.

Riis and Mrs. Riis (together, starting up from their chairs). You, Svava?

Svava. I was quite young at the time. Like most young girls, I was looking for my ideal, and found it in a young, vivacious man—I won't describe him more accurately. He had—oh, the noblest principles and the highest aims —the most complete contrast to you in that respect, father! To say I loved him, is much too mild; I worshipped him. But I never can tell you what I discovered, or how I discovered it. It was the time when you all thought I had—

Mrs. Riis. —something wrong with your lungs? Is it possible, child? Was it then?

Svava. Yes, it was then.—No one could endure or forgive being deceived like that!

Mrs. Riis. And you never said a word to me?

Svava. Only those who have made such a mistake as I did can understand the shame one feels.—Well, it is all over now. But this much is certain, that no one who has had such an experience once will make the same mistake again. (*Meanwhile Riis has gone into his room.*)

Mrs. Riis. Perhaps it was a good thing for you, after all?

Svava. I am sure it was.—Well, it is all done with now. But it was not quite done with till I found Alfred. Where is father?

Mrs. Riis. Your father? Here he comes.

Riis (coming out of his room, with his hat on, and drawing on his gloves). Look here, little girl! I must go and see what has happened to my luggage at the Customs. I will go to the station and telegraph. You must have all your things looking very nice, you know, because the King is coming here in a day or two—and so it is worth it! Good-bye, then, my dear girl! (*Kisses her.*) You have made us very happy—so very happy. It is true you have certain ideas that are not—. Well, never mind! Good-bye! (*Goes out.*)

Mrs. Riis. Good-bye!

Riis (*drawing off his gloves*). Did you notice the tune I was playing when you came in? (*Sits down at the piano.*) I heard it everywhere in Germany. (*Begins to play and sing, but stops short.*) But, bless my soul, here is the music! You can play it and sing it for yourself. (*Goes out, humming the air.*)

Svava. He is delightful! There is really something so innocent about him. Did you notice him yesterday? He was simply coruscating.

Mrs. Riis. You did not see yourself, my dear!

Svava. Why? Was I sparkling, too?

Mrs. Riis. Your father's daughter—absolutely!

Svava. Yes, it is no use denying, mother, that however great one's happiness is, the friendliness of others increases it. I was thinking to-day over all the things that gave me so much happiness yesterday, and felt—oh, I can't tell you what I felt! (*Nestles in her mother's arms.*)

Mrs. Riis. You are a very lucky girl!—Now I must go and do my housekeeping.

Svava. Shall I help you?

Mrs. Riis. No, thank you, dear. (*They cross the room together.*)

Svava. Well, then, I will run through father's song once or twice—and Alfred should be here directly. (MRS. RIIS *goes out by the door on the left.* SVAVA *sits down at the piano.* ALFRED *comes in softly from the left, and bends over her shoulder so that his face comes close to hers.*)

Alfred. Good morning, darling!

Svava (*jumping up*). Alfred! I did not hear the door!

Alfred. Because you were playing. Something very pretty, too!

Svava. I enjoyed myself so much yesterday!

Alfred. I do not believe you have any idea what an impression you made!

Svava. Just a suspicion. But you must not talk about that, because it would be most improper for me to confess it!

Alfred. Every one was singing your praises to me, and to mother and father too. We are all very happy at home to-day.

Svava. So we are here!—What is that you have got in your hand? A letter?

Alfred. Yes, a letter. Your maid who opened the door gave it to me. Some one has been clever enough to count upon my coming here some time this morning.

Svava. You don't think that was difficult to guess?

Alfred. Not particularly. It is from Edward Hansen.

Svava. But you can take a short cut to his house through our park. (*Points to the right.*)

Alfred. Yes, I know. And as he says it is urgent, and underlines the word—

Svava. —you can have my key. Here it is. (*Gives it to him.*)

Alfred. Thank you, dear, very much.

Svava. Oh, it is only selfishness; we shall have you back again all the sooner.

Alfred. I will stay here till lunch time.

Svava. You will stay here a great deal longer than that. We have a frightful lot to talk about—all about yesterday, and—

Alfred. Of course we have!

Svava. And lots of other things as well.

Alfred. I have a most important question to ask you.

Svava. Have you?

Alfred. Perhaps you will find the answer by the time I come back.

Svava. It can't be so very difficult, then!

Alfred. Indeed it is. But sometimes you have inspirations.

Svava. What is it?

Alfred. Why did we two not find each other many years ago?

Svava. Because we were not ready for it, of course!

Alfred. How do you know that?

Svava. Because I know that at that time I was quite another girl from what I am now.

Alfred. But there is a natural affinity between those that love one another. I am sure of it. And it was just as much the case at that time, surely?

Svava. We do not feel the natural affinity as long as we are developing on different lines.

Alfred. Have we been doing that? And nevertheless we—

Svava. Nevertheless we love one another. Our paths may be as unlike as they please, if only they lead together in the end.

Alfred. To the same way of thinking, you mean?

Svava. Yes, to our being such comrades as we are now.

Alfred. Such true comrades?

Svava. Such true comrades!

Alfred. Still, it is just at moments like this, when I hold you in my arms as I do now, that I ask myself over and over again why I did not do this long ago.

Svava. Oh, I don't think about that—not the least bit! It is the safest place in the world—that is what I think!

Alfred. Perhaps before this year it would not have been so.

Svava. What do you mean?

Alfred. I mean—well, I mean practically the same as you; that I have not always been the man I am now.— But I must hurry away. The letter says it is something urgent. (*They cross the room together*.)

Svava. One minute won't make any difference, will it? —because there is something I must say to you first.

Alfred (*standing still*). What is it?

Svava. When I saw you standing amongst all the others yesterday, I felt for the first moment as if I did not know you. Some change seemed to have come over you—the effect of the others, perhaps—anyway you really *were* actually different.

Alfred. Of course. People always are that, among strangers. When you came in with the ladies, it just seemed to me as if I had never observed you carefully before. Besides, there are certain things one cannot know till one sees a person amongst others. It was the first time I realised how tall you are—and your way of bending just a tiny bit to one side when you bow to any one. And your colouring! I had never properly seen—

Svava. Do be quiet, and let me get a word in!

Alfred. No, no! Here we are, back in the room—and I *must* be off now!

Svava. Only just a moment. You interrupted me, you know! When I saw you standing there among the men, for the first moment I felt just as if I did not know you. But at the same moment you caught sight of me and nodded. I don't know what sort of a transformation came over us both; but I felt myself blushing as red as fire. And it was some time before I had the courage to look at you again.

Alfred. Well, do you know what happened to me? Every time any one came to dance with you, didn't I envy him! Oh, not at all!—To tell you the truth, I cannot bear any one else to touch you. (*Clasps her in his arms.*) And I have not told you the best part of it yet.

Svava. What is that?

Alfred. That when I see you amongst other people, and catch—say—a glimpse of your arm, I think to myself: That arm has been round my neck and round no one else's in the whole world! She is mine, mine, mine—and no one else's!—There, that is the best part of it all!—Look here, here we are back again in the room! It is witchcraft! Now I *must* go. (*Crosses the room.*) Good-bye! (*Lets her go, then catches hold of her again.*) Why didn't I find my happiness many years ago?—Good-bye!

Svava. I think I will come with you.

Alfred. Yes, do!

Svava. No, I forgot—I must learn this song before father comes back. If I don't learn it now, I expect you will take care I don't do so to-day. (*A ring is heard at the front door.*)

Alfred. Here is some one coming! Let me get away first. (*Hurries out to the right.* SVAVA *stands waving her hand to him, then turns to the piano. The maid* MARGIT *enters.*)

Margit. A gentleman has called, miss, who wants to know if—

Svava. A gentleman? Don't you know who he is?

Margit. No, miss.

Svava. What is he like?

Margit. He looks rather—

Svava. Rather suspicious?

Margit. No, far from it, miss—a very nice gentleman.

Svava. Tell him my father is not at home; he has gone down to the station.

Margit. I told him so, miss, but it is you he wants to see.

Svava. Ask my mother to come in here!—Oh, no, why should she! Let him come in. (MARGIT *shows in* HOFF, *and goes out.*)

Hoff. Is it Miss Riis I have the honour to—? Yes, I see it is. My name is Hoff—Karl Hoff. I am a commercial traveller—travel in iron.

Svava. But what has that to do with me?

Hoff. Just this much, that if I had been an ordinary stay-at-home man, a great many things would not have happened.

Svava. What would not have happened?

Hoff (*taking a large pocket-book out of his pocket, and extracting a letter from it*). Will you condescend to read this? Or perhaps you would rather not?

Svava. How can I tell?

Hoff. Of course, you must first— Allow me. (*Gives her the letter.*)

Svava (*reading*). "To-night between ten and eleven; that is to say, if the booby has not come home. I love you so dearly! Put a light in the hall window."

Hoff. "The booby" is me.

Svava. But I don't understand—?

Hoff. Here is another.

Svava. "I am full of remorse. Your cough frightens me; and now, when you are expecting—" But what in the world has this to do with me?

Hoff (*after a moment's thought*). What do you suppose?

Svava. Is it some one you want me to help?

Hoff. No, poor soul, she doesn't need help any more. She is dead.

Svava. Dead? Was she your wife?

Hoff. That's it. She was my wife. I found these and some other things in a little box. At the bottom were these notes—there are more of them—and some cotton wool on the top of them. On the top of that lay some earrings and things that had been her mother's. And also (*producing some bracelets*) these bracelets. They are certainly much too costly to have been her mother's.

Svava. I suppose she died suddenly, as she did not—

Hoff. I cannot say. Consumptives never think they are going to die. Anyway she was very delicate and weak.—May I sit down?

Svava. Please do. Are there any children?

Hoff (*after a moment's thought*). I believe not.

Svava. You believe not? I asked because I thought you wanted our Society to help you. This really is all very distressful to me.

Hoff. I thought it would be—I thought as much. Besides, I am not really sure if I—. You cannot understand this, then?

Svava. No, I cannot.

Hoff. No, you cannot.—I have heard so much good spoken of you for many years. My wife used to sing your praises, too.

Svava. Did she know me?

Hoff. She was Maren Tang—who used to be companion to—

Svava. —to Mrs. Christensen, my future mother-in-law? Was it she? She was such a well-bred, quiet woman. Are you sure you are not mistaken? One or two notes, unsigned and undated—what?

Hoff. Did you not recognise the handwriting?

Svava. I? No. Besides, isn't it a disguised hand?

Hoff. Yes, but not much disguised.

Svava. I presume you had some more definite errand with me?

Hoff. Yes, I had—but I think I will let it alone. You do not understand anything about this, I can see. Perhaps you think I am a little crazy? I am not so sure you would not be right.

Svava. But there was something you wanted to say to me?

Hoff. Yes, there was. You see, these Kindergartens—

Svava. Oh, so it was them, all the time?

Hoff. No, it was not them. But they are responsible for my having for a long time thought very highly of you, Miss Riis. If you will excuse my saying so, I had never before seen fashionable young ladies trying to do anything useful—never. I am only a little broken-down tradesman, travelling for a firm—a worthless sort of chap in many ways, and one that very likely deserves what he has got —but anyway I wanted *you* to be spared. Indeed I thought it was my duty—absolutely my duty. But now, when I see you sitting there before me—well, now I only feel miserably unhappy. So I won't trouble you at all. (*Gets up.*) Not at all.

Svava. I really cannot understand—

Hoff. Please don't bother about me! And please forgive my disturbing you.—No, you really must not give me another thought! Just imagine that I have not been here—that is all. (*As he reaches the door, he meets* ALFRED *coming in. As soon as he sees that* SVAVA *is watching them, he goes hurriedly out.* SVAVA *sees the meeting between the two and gives a little scream, then rushes to meet* ALFRED. *But as soon as she is face to face with him, she seems terrified. As he comes nearer to take her in his arms she cries out:* "Don't touch me!" *and hurries out by the door on the left.*

She is heard locking and bolting it on the inside. Then a violent outburst of weeping is heard, the sound being somewhat deadened by the distance, but only for a few moments. Then the sound of singing is heard outside, and a few seconds later RIIS *comes into the room. The curtain falls as he enters.*)

ACT II

(SCENE.—*The same as in Act I. SVAVA is lying on the couch to the right, resting her head on one hand and looking out towards the park. Her mother is sitting beside her.*)

Mrs. Riis. Decisions as hasty as yours, Svava, are not really decisions at all. There is always a great deal more to be taken into consideration than one realises at first. Take time to think it over! I believe he is a fine fellow. Give him time to show it; don't break it off immediately!

Svava. Why do you keep on saying that to me?

Mrs. Riis. Well, dear, you know I have never had the chance of saying anything to you till to-day.

Svava. But you keep harping on that one string.

Mrs. Riis. What note do you want me to strike, then?

Svava. The note your dear good mother would have struck—quite a different one altogether.

Mrs. Riis. It is one thing to teach your child how to make a proper choice in life, but—

Svava. But quite another thing to put into practice what you teach?

Mrs. Riis. No; I was going to say that life itself is quite another thing. In daily life, and especially in married life, it is sometimes advisable to make allowances.

Svava. Yes, on points that do not really matter.

Mrs. Riis. Only on points that do not matter?

136

Svava. Yes—personal peculiarities, and things like that, which after all are only excrescences; but not on points that concern one's moral growth.

Mrs. Riis. Yes, on those points too.

Svava. On those points too?—But isn't it just for the sake of our own self-development that we marry? What else should we marry for?

Mrs. Riis. Oh, you will see!

Svava. No, indeed I shall not; because I do not intend to marry on such conditions.

Mrs. Riis. You should have said that sooner. It is too late now.

Svava (sitting upright). Too late? If I had been married twenty years, I would have done just the same! (*Lies down again.*)

Mrs. Riis. Heaven help you, then!—You haven't an idea, not the smallest idea, what a net you are entangled in! But you will find it out, as soon as you begin to struggle in earnest. Or do you really want your father and me to throw away all that we have worked for here?— to begin all over again in a foreign country? Because he has repeatedly said, during the last day or two, that he will not be mixed up in the scandal that would be the result of your breaking this off. He would go abroad, and I should have to go with him. Ah, you wince at the thought of that!—Think of all your friends, too. It is a serious matter to have been set on such an eminence as you were at your betrothal party. It is like being lifted up high on a platform that others are carrying on their shoulders; take care you do not fall down from it! That is what you will do, if you offend their principles of right behaviour.

Svava. Is that sort of thing a principle of right behaviour?

Mrs. Riis. I do not say that. But undoubtedly, one of their principles of right behaviour—and perhaps the most important—is that all scandal must be avoided. No one relishes being disgraced, Svava—particularly the most influential people in a place. And least of all, by a long way, do people relish their own child being disgraced.

Svava (half raising herself). Good Lord! is it *I* that am disgracing *him?*

Mrs. Riis. No, of course, it is he himself—

Svava. Very well, then! (*Sinks down upon the couch again.*)

Mrs. Riis. But you will never get them to understand that. I assure you, you won't. As long as what he has done is only whispered about in his family and amongst his intimate friends, they don't consider him disgraced at all. There are too many that do just the same. It is only when the knowledge of it becomes common property, that they consider it a disgrace. And if it became known that there was a formal breach between you—the Christensens' eldest son ignominiously refused because of his past life—they would consider it the most shocking scandal that could possibly overtake them! And we should feel the effect of it, in particular. And so would those that are dependent on us—and they are not so few in number, as you know, because you have interested yourself in them, particularly in the children. You would have to give up all the interests you have made for yourself here—because you would have to go with us. I am certain your father is in earnest about that.

Svava. Oh! Oh!

Mrs. Riis. I almost wish I could tell you why I am so certain of that. But I cannot—at all events not now. No, you must not tempt me to.—Here comes your father. Only take time to reflect, Svava! No breaking of it off, no scandal! (Riis *comes in from outside, with an opened letter in his hand.*)

Riis. Oh, there you are! (*Goes into his room, lays down his hat and stick, and comes out again.*) You have taken no serious step yet, I hope—eh?

Mrs. Riis. No, but—

Riis. Very well. Now here is a letter from the Christensens. If you won't receive either your *fiancé* or his letters, you will have to put up with his family's interference in the matter. Everything must come to an end sooner or later. (*Reads.*) "My wife, my son and I will do ourselves the honour of paying you a visit between eleven and twelve o'clock." The only wonder is, that I have not had some such letter before this! I am sure they have been patient enough.

Mrs. Riis. Well, we have got no farther to-day, either.

Riis. What are you thinking of, child? Can't you see what it must all lead to? You are a good-hearted girl, I know—I am sure you don't want to ruin us all absolutely? I certainly consider, Svava, that you have acted quite severely enough now in this matter. They have suffered a nasty shock to their self-confidence, both of them; you may be quite sure of that. What more do you want? If you are really determined to carry the matter farther—well—make your conditions! There is no doubt they will be agreed to.

Svava. For shame! For shame!

Riis (*despairingly*). What is the use of taking it in this way!

Mrs. Riis. What, indeed! You ought rather to try and make things a bit easier, Svava.

Riis. And you really might condescend, too, to consider who it is that you are throwing over—a member of one of the richest families in the country, and, I venture to say, one of the most honourable too. I have never heard of anything so idiotic! Yes, I repeat—idiotic, idiotic! What if he have made a false step—or two—well, good heavens—

Svava. Yes, bring heaven into it, too!

Riis. Indeed I well may! There is good need. As I was saying, if he have made a false step, surely the poor fellow has been sufficiently punished for it now. Besides, it is certainly our duty to be a little reasonable with one another—it is a commandment, you know, that we are to be reasonable and forgiving. We must be forgiving! And more than that, we must help the erring—we must raise up the fallen and set them in the right way. Yes, set them in the right way. You could do that so splendidly! It is exactly in your line. You know very well, my dear child, it is very seldom I talk about morals and that sort of thing. It doesn't sit well on me at all; I know that only too well. But on this occasion I cannot help it. Begin with forgiveness, my child; begin with that! After all, can you contemplate living together with any one for any length of time without—without—well, without *that?*

Svava. But there is no question of living with any one for any length of time, or of forgiveness—because I do not mean to have anything more to do with him.

Riis. Really, this is beyond all bounds! Because he has dared to fall in love with some one before you—?

Svava. Some one?

Riis. Well, if there was more than one, I am sure I know nothing about it. No, indeed I do not! Besides, the way people gossip and backbite is the very devil! But, as I was saying, because he dared to look at some one before he looked at you—before he ever *thought* of you— is that a reason for throwing him over for good and all?

How many would ever get married under those circumstances, I should like to know? Everybody confirms the opinion that he is an honourable, fine young fellow, to whom the proudest girl might confidently entrust herself —you said so yourself, only a day or two ago! Do not deny it! And now he is suddenly to be thrown over, because you are not the first girl he has ever met! Pride should have some limits, remember! I have never heard of anything more preposterous, if you ask me.

Mrs. Riis. Men are not like that.

Riis. And what about girls? Are they like that? I am quite sure they do not ask whether their *fiancés* have been married before—observe, I said "married." You can imagine he has been married. Well, why not? That is what other girls do—you cannot deny it. I know you know it. You have been to dances; who are most in request there? Precisely those who have the reputation of being something of a Don Juan. They take the wind out of all the other fellows' sails. You have seen it yourself a hundred times. And it is not only at dances that this applies. Don't you suppose they get married— and as a rule make the very best matches?

Mrs. Riis. That is true.

Riis. Of course it is true. And as a rule they make the very best husbands, too!

Mrs. Riis. Hm!

Riis. Oh, indeed they do!—with some exceptions, of course, naturally. The fact is, that marriage has an ennobling influence, and provides a beautiful vocation for a woman—the most beautiful vocation possible!

Svava (*who has got up*). I can just manage to listen to such things from you—because I expected no better from you.

Riis. Thank you very much!

Svava (who has come forward). One would really think that marriage were a sort of superior wash-house for men—

Riis. Ha, ha!

Svava. —and that men could come there and take a dip when they please—and in what state they please!

Riis. Oh, really—!

Svava. I mean it! And it is flattering—very flattering —for me, as your daughter, to feel that you look upon me as so peculiarly suited for the washerwoman's post! None of that for me, thank you!

Riis. But this is—

Svava. No, just listen to me for a little! I don't think I have said too much, the last day or two.

Riis. No, we have not been allowed to say a word to you.

Svava. Look here, father. You have a fine supply of principles, for show purposes.

Riis. For—?

Svava. I do not mean by that, that they are not your own. But you are so good and so honourable, your whole life is so refined, that I do not attach the least importance to your principles. But to mother's I do attach importance, for hers are what have formed mine. And now, just when I want to act up to them, she deserts me.

Riis and Mrs. Riis (together). Svava!

Svava. It is mother I am angry with! It is mother I cannot have patience with!

Riis. Really, Svava—!

Svava. Because if there has been one point on which mother and I have been agreed, it has been on the subject of the unprincipled way men prepare themselves for marriage, and the sort of marriages that are the result. We have watched the course of it, mother and I, for many years; and we had come to one and the same conclusion, that it is *before* marriage that a marriage is marred. But when, the other day, mother began to turn round—

Mrs. Riis. No, you have no right to say that! I am convinced that Alfred is as honourable—

Svava. But when, the other day, mother began to turn round—well, I could not have been more amazed if some one had come in and told me they had met her out in the street when she was actually sitting here talking to me.

Mrs. Riis. I only ask you to take time to consider! I am not contradicting you!

Svava. Oh, let me speak now! Let me give you just one instance. One day, before I was really grown up, I came running into this room from the park. We had just bought the property, and I was so happy. Mother was standing over there leaning against the door and crying. It was a lovely summer's day. "Why are you crying, mother?" I said. For some time she seemed as if she did not see me. "Why are you crying, mother?" I repeated, and went nearer to her, but did not like to touch her. She turned away from me, and walked up and down once or twice. Then she came to me. "My child," she said, drawing me to her, "never give in to what is not good and pure, on any account whatever! It is so cowardly, and one repents it so bitterly; it means perpetually giving in, more and more and more." I do not know what she referred to, and I have never asked. But no one can imagine what an effect it all had on me—the beautiful summer day, and mother crying, and the heartfelt tones of her voice! I cannot give in; do not ask me to. Everything that made marriage seem beautiful to me is gone—my faith, my feeling of security—all gone! No, no, no! I can never begin with that, and it is wicked of you to want to make me believe I can. After such a disillusionment and such a humiliation? No! I would rather never be married—even if I have to go away from here. I daresay I shall find something to fill my life; it is only for the moment that I feel so helpless. And anything is better than to fill it with what is unclean. If I did not refuse that without hesitation, I should be an accomplice to it. Perhaps some people could put up with that. I cannot—no, I cannot! Do you think it is arrogance on my part? Or because I am angry? If you knew what we two had planned and schemed, you would understand me. And if you knew what I have thought of him, how I have admired him— you did the same yourselves—and how wretched I feel now, how utterly robbed of everything!—Who is it that is crying? Is it you, mother? (*She runs to her mother, kneels down and buries her head in her lap. A pause.* RIIS *goes into his room.*) Why cannot we three hold together? If we do, what have we to be afraid of? What is it that stands in the way? Father, what is it that stands in the way?—But where is father? (*Sees* NORDAN *outside the window.*) Uncle Nordan! This is a surprise! (*Hurries across the room, throws herself into* NORDAN'S *arms as he enters, and bursts into tears.*)

Nordan. Oh, you goose! You great goose!

Svava. You must come and talk to me!

Nordan. Isn't that what I am here for?

Svava. And I thought you were up in the mountains and could not hear from us.

Nordan. So I was. But when I got telegram after telegram, as long as they could reach me, and then one express letter after another—and now the end of it all is—well, I don't suppose I dare even mention his name here now? (RIIS *comes in from his room.*)

Riis. At last! We have been so anxious for you to come!

Mrs. Riis (*who has at last risen and come forward*). Thank you for coming, dear doctor!

Nordan (*looking at her*). There is something serious up, then?

Mrs. Riis. I have something I want to say to you.

Nordan. Yes, but just now away you go, you two! Let me talk to this booby. (MRS. RIIS *goes out to the left.* SVAVA *follows her for a minute.*)

Riis. I just want to tell you that in a little while—

Nordan. —the whole pack of Christensens will be here? I know that. Go away now.

Riis. Nordan! (*Whispers to him.*)

Nordan. Yes, yes!—Quite so!—No, of course not! (*Tries to stop his whispering.*) Do you suppose I don't know what I am about? Be off with you! (SVAVA *comes in, as her father goes out.*)

Svava. Dear Uncle Nordan! At last, somebody that will agree with me!

Nordan. Am I?

Svava. Oh, Uncle Nordan, you don't know what these days have been like!

Nordan. And the nights too, I expect?—although, with all that, you don't look so bad.

Svava. The last night or two I have slept.

Nordan. Really? Then I see how things stand. You are a tough customer, you are!

Svava. Oh, don't begin saying a lot of things you don't mean, uncle.

Nordan. Things I don't mean!

Svava. You always do, you know. But we haven't time for that now. I am all on fire!

Nordan. Well, what is this you have been doing?

K

Svava. Ah, you see, you are beginning again!

Nordan. Beginning again? Who the devil has put the idea into your head that I ever say anything but what I mean? Come and let us sit down. (*Brings a chair forward.*)

Svava (*bringing her chair close to his*). There now!

Nordan. Since I was here last, I believe you have promulgated a brand-new law on the subject of love? I congratulate you.

Svava. Have I?

Nordan. A superhuman, Svava - woven one—derived from seraphic heights, I should imagine! "There shall be only one love in a man's life, and it shall be directed only to one object." Full stop!

Svava. Have I said anything like that?

Nordan. Is it not you that have thrown over a young man because he has had the audacity to fall in love before he saw you?

Svava. Do you take it in that way, too?

Nordan. In that way? Is there any other way for a sensible man to take it? A fine young fellow honestly adores you; a distinguished family throw their doors wide open to you, as if you were a princess; and then you turn round and say: "You have not waited for me ever since you were a child! Away with you!"

Svava (*springing up*). What, you too! You too! And the same talk! The same stupid talk!

Nordan. I can tell you what it is; if you do not give consideration to everything that can be said on the other side, *you* are stupid.—No, it is no use going away from me and marching up and down! I shall begin and march up and down too, if you do! Come here and sit. Or *daren't* you go thoroughly into the question with me?

Svava. Yes, I dare. (*Sits down again.*)

Nordan. Well, to begin with, do you not think there must certainly be two sides to a question that is discussed by serious men and women all over the world?

Svava. This only concerns me! And as far as I am concerned there is only one side to it.

Nordan. You do not understand me, child! You shall settle your own affairs ultimately, and nobody else—of course. But suppose what you have to settle is not quite so simple as you think it? Suppose it is a problem that at the present moment is exercising the minds of thousands and thousands of people? Do you not think it is your duty to give some consideration to the usual attitude towards it, and to what is generally thought and said about it? Do you think it is conscientious to condemn in a single instance without doing that?

Svava. I understand! I think I have done what you are urging me to do. Ask mother!

Nordan. Oh, I daresay you and your mother have chattered and read a lot about marriage and the woman question, and about abolishing distinctions of class—now you want to abolish distinctions of sex too. But as regards this special question?

Svava. What do you consider I have overlooked?

Nordan. Just this. Are you right in being equally as strict with men as with women? Eh?

Svava. Yes, of course.

Nordan. Is it so much a matter of course? Go out and ask any one you meet. Out of every hundred you ask, ninety will say " no "—even out of a hundred women!

Svava. Do you think so? I think people are beginning to think otherwise.

Nordan. Possibly. But experience is necessary if one is to answer a question like that.

Svava. Do you mean what you say?

Nordan. That is none of your business. Besides, I always mean what I say.—A woman can marry when she is sixteen; a man must wait till he is five-and-twenty, or thirty. There is a difference.

Svava. There *is* a difference! There are many, many times more unmarried women than men, and they exhibit self-control. Men find it more convenient to make a law of their want of self-control!

Nordan. An answer like that only displays your ignorance. Man is a polygamous animal, like many other animals—a theory that is very strongly supported by the fact that women so outnumber men in the world. I daresay that is something you have never heard before?

Svava. Yes, I have heard it!

Nordan. Don't you laugh at science! What else are we to put faith in, I should like to know?

Svava. I should just like men to have the same trouble over their children that women do! Just let them have that, Uncle Nordan, and I fancy they would soon change their principles! Just let them experience it!

Nordan. They have no time for that; they have to govern the world.

Svava. Yes, they have allotted the parts themselves!— Now, tell me this, Dr. Nordan. Is it cowardly not to practise what you preach?

Nordan. Of course it is.

Svava. Then why do you not do it?

Nordan. I? I have always been a regular monster. Don't you know that, dear child?

Svava. Dear Uncle Nordan—you have such long white locks; why do you wear them like that?

Nordan. Oh, well—I have my reasons.

Svava. What are they?

Nordan. We won't go into that now.

Svava. You told me the reason once.

Nordan. Did I?

Svava. I wanted, one day, to take hold of your hair, but you would not let me. You said: "Do you know why you must not do that?"—"No," I said.—"Because no one has done that for more than thirty years."—"Who was it that did it last?" I asked.—"It was a little girl, that you are very like," you answered.

Nordan. So I told you that, did I?

Svava. "And she was one of your grandmother's younger sisters," you said to me.

Nordan. She was. It was quite true. And you are like her, my child.

Svava. And then you told me that the year you went to college she was standing beside you one day and caught up some locks of your hair in her fingers. "You must never wear your hair shorter than this," she said. She went away, and you went away; and when, one day, you wrote and asked her whether you two did not belong to one another, her answer was "yes." And a month later she was dead.

Nordan. She was dead.

Svava. And ever since then—you dear, queer old uncle —you have considered yourself as married to her. (*He nods.*) And ever since the evening you told me that— and I lay awake a long time, thinking over it—I wanted, even when I was quite a young girl, to choose some one I could have perfect confidence in. And then I chose wrong.

Nordan. Did you, Svava?

Svava. Do not ask me any more about that.—Then I chose once again, and this time I was certain! For never had truer eyes looked in mine. And how happy we were together! Day after day it always seemed new, and the days were always too short. I dare not think about it now. Oh, it is sinful to deceive us so!—not deceit in words, it is true, but in letting us give them our admiration and our most intimate confidences. Not in words, no— and yet, it is in words; because they accept all we say, and are silent themselves, and by that very fact make our words their own. Our simple-mindedness pleases them as a bit of unspoilt nature, and it is just by means of that that they deceive us. It creates an intimacy between us and an atmosphere of happy give-and-take of jests, which we think can exist only on one presupposition—and really it is all a sham. I cannot understand how any one can so treat the one he loves—for he did love me!

Nordan. He does love you.

Svava (getting up). But not as I loved him! All these years I have not been frittering away my love. Besides, I have had too high an ideal of what loving and being loved should be; and just for that reason I felt a deep desire to be loved—I can say so to you. And when love came, it seemed to take all my strength from me; but I felt I should always be safe with him, and so I let him see it and gloried in his seeing it. That is the bitterest part of it to me now—because he was unworthy of it. He has said to me: " I cannot bear to see any one else touch you! " and " When I catch a glimpse of your arm, I think to myself that it has been round my neck—mine, and no one else's in the world." And I felt proud and happy when he said so, because I thought it was true. Hundreds of times I had imagined some one's saying that to me some day. But I never imagined that the one who would say it would be a man who—oh, it is disgusting! When I think what it means, it makes me ready to hate him! The mere thought that he has had his arms round me— has touched me—makes me shudder! I am not laying down rules for any one else, but what I am doing seems to me a matter of course. Every fibre of my being tells me that. I must be left in peace!

Nordan. I see that this is more serious, and goes deeper, than I had any suspicion of. None of them understand it that way, Alfred least of all. He is only hurt—distressed and hurt at the thought that you could distrust him.

Svava. I know that.

Nordan. Yes—well—don't take up such a high and mighty attitude! I assure you that is how it will appear to most people.

Svava. Do you think so? I think people are beginning to think otherwise.

Nordan. Most people will think: " Other girls forgive things like that, especially when they love a man."

Svava. There are some that will answer: " If she had not loved him, she might have forgiven him."

Nordan. And yet, Svava?—and yet?

Svava. But, uncle, do you not understand? I do not know that I can explain it, either; because, to do that, I should have to explain what it is that we read into the face, the character, the manner of the man we love—his voice, his smile. That is what I have lost. Its meaning is gone.

Nordan. For a while, yes—till you have had a breathing space.

Svava. No, no, no! Do you remember that song of mine, about the beloved one's image? that one always sees it as if it were framed in happiness? Do you remember it?

Nordan. Yes.

Svava. Very well—I cannot see it like that any longer. I see it, of course—but always with pain. Always! Am I to forgive that, because other girls forgive it? What is that they have loved, these other girls? Can you tell me that? Because what I loved is gone. I am not going to sit down and try to conjure it up in my imagination again. I shall find something else to do.

Nordan. You are embittered now. You have had your ideal thoroughly shattered, and as long as you are smarting from that it is no use reasoning with you. So I will only beg one thing of you—one single little thing. But you must promise me to do it?

Svava. If I can.

Nordan. You can. There are things to take into consideration. Ask for time to think it all over!

Svava. Ah!—mother has been writing to you!

Nordan. And if she has? Your mother knows what depends upon it.

Svava. What depends upon it? Why do you speak so mysteriously, as if we were not on secure ground? Aren't we? Father talks about giving up this place. Why?

Nordan. I suppose he thinks it will be necessary.

Svava. Father? On grounds of economy?

Nordan. Not in the least! No, but all the gossips in the place will be at you. What you propose to do is a regular challenge, you know.

Svava. Oh, we can stand criticism! Father has some queer principles, you know; but his own life—. Surely no one has any doubt about that?

Nordan. Listen to me, my child. You cannot prevent people inventing things. So be careful!

Svava. What do you mean?

Nordan. I mean that you ought to go for a stroll in the park and pull yourself together a little, before the Christensens come. Try to be calm; come in calmly, and request time to think it over. That is all you have to do! They will make no difficulty about that, because they must agree. Nothing has happened yet, and all ways are still open. Do as I ask!

Svava. I *have* thought it over—and you will never get me to do anything else.

Nordan. No, no. It is only a matter of form.

Svava. What? You mean something more than that, I know.

Nordan. What an obstinate girl you are!—Can you not do it then, let me say, for your mother's sake? Your mother is a good woman.

Svava. What will they think, if I come in and say: "Will you not give me time to consider the matter?" No, I cannot do that.

Nordan. What will you say, then?

Svava. I would rather say nothing at all. But if I absolutely must say something—

Nordan. Of course you must!

Svava. Well, I will go out now and think it over. (*Turns to go, but stops.*) But what you want can never be.

Nordan. It *must* be!

Svava (*standing by the door*). You said just now: "Your mother is a good woman." It sounded almost as if you laid stress on the word "mother"?

Nordan. Suppose I did?

Svava. Is father not that, too?

Nordan. Your father a good woman?

Svava. Why do you try to turn it off with a joke?

Nordan. Because it is serious, confound it all!

Svava. Can I not believe father—?

Nordan. Hush!

Svava. Father?—Is it possible that he too—? Do people say that? (NORDAN *does not answer, and does not move.*) Shameful! Impossible! I say it is impossible! (*Rushes out.* RIIS *comes in from the right.*)

Riis. What is the matter with Svava?

Nordan (*coming forward*). There was nothing else for it.

Riis. Nothing else for it? What do you mean?

Nordan. No, devil take it!—there was nothing else for it.

Riis. Quite so—but what?

Nordan. What do you say?

Riis. No, what were *you* saying—?

Nordan. What was *I* saying?

Riis. You said there was nothing else for it. You alarm me.

Nordan. Do I? Then you did not hear right. (*Moves away from him.*)

Riis. Didn't hear right? You were swearing about it, too!

Nordan. That I certainly did not.

Riis. Very well then, you didn't. But how did you get on with Svava? Won't you answer me?

Nordan. How did I get on with Svava?

Riis. Why are you so preoccupied? Are things so bad, then?

Nordan. Preoccupied? Why should I be that?

Riis. You ought to know best. I was asking about Svava—how you got on with Svava—and I think I have the right to know.

Nordan. Look here, Riis.

Riis. Yes? (NORDAN *takes him by the arm.*) What is it?

Nordan. Did you see Svava?

Riis. Hurrying away out through the park? Yes. My dear chap, what was it?

Nordan. It was the Greek tragedy.

Riis. The Greek—?

Nordan. Only the name—only the name! Well, you know what the word means, don't you?

Riis. The Greek—?

Nordan. No, no—not " Greek," but " tragedy "?

Riis. Something mournful—?

Nordan. Far from it! Something amusing! It came to Greece with the worship of Dionysus, in whose train there was a goat—

Riis (draws his arm away). A goat? What on earth—?

Nordan. Yes, you may well be surprised—because it sang!

Riis. Sang?

Nordan. Yes—and is still singing, of course! And paints! There are pictures by him in every exhibition. And works in bronze and marble! Wonderful! And such a courtier as he is, too! It is he that designs ball-dresses and arranges entertainments—

Riis. Have you gone raving mad?

Nordan. Why do you ask that?

Riis. I am waiting patiently here till you have done talking such damned nonsense! We are accustomed to something of the sort when you are in one of those humours, but to-day I can't understand a blessed word of what you are saying.

Nordan. Don't you, my dear fellow?

Riis. Can you not tell me what my daughter said? Isn't it ridiculous that I cannot get that out of you! Now, briefly and intelligibly, what did she say?

Nordan. Do you want to know?

Riis. He asks that!

Nordan. She said she pitied all the innocent young girls that, generation after generation, disappear—

Riis. Where to?

Nordan. That is just it—where to? She said: " They

are brought up in pious ignorance, and finally the unsuspecting creatures are wrapped up in a long white veil so that they shall not be able to see distinctly where they are being taken to."

Riis. Now you are talking your mythology again. Am I not to—

Nordan. Be quiet! It is your daughter that is speaking. "But I will not do that," she said. "I will enter confidently into the holy estate of matrimony, and sit down by the hearth in the land of my fathers, and bring up children in the sight of my husband. But he shall be as chaste as I; for otherwise he stains my child's head, when he kisses it, and dishonours me."—There, that is what she said, and she looked so splendid as she said it. (*A ring is heard at the bell.*)

Riis. They are upon us! They are upon us! What in the world is going to happen? We are in a muddle of the most preposterous theories! The whole heathen mythology is buzzing round in my head! (*Hurries to the door to meet* MR. *and* MRS. CHRISTENSEN, *whom* MARGIT *is showing in.*) I am so happy to see you!—so very happy! But your son?

Christensen. We could not get him to come with us.

Riis. I am very sorry!—At the same time, I quite understand.

Christensen. I admire the beauty of this place afresh every time I see it, my dear sir!

Mrs. Christensen. This beautiful old park! I wanted once—. Oh, good morning, doctor! How are you?

Nordan. So, so!

Riis (*to* MARGIT). Please tell Mrs. Riis. And—oh, there she is. (MRS. RIIS *comes in by the door at the left.*) And tell Miss Svava.

Nordan. She is out in the park (*pointing*)—out that way. (*Exit* MARGIT.)

Riis. No, this way!—That's right! Go straight on till you find her.

Mrs. Christensen (*who meantime has come forward with* MRS. RIIS). I have been thinking so much about you the last day or two, my dear! What a tiresome business this is!

Mrs. Riis. Do you mind my asking if you knew anything about it before?

Mrs. Christensen. What is there that a mother—and a wife—escapes the knowledge of nowadays, my dear! She was in my service, you know. Come here! (*Tells* MRS. RIIS *something in a whisper, ending with something about* "discovery" *and* "dismissal.")

Riis (*offering the ladies chairs*). Won't you sit down?— Oh, I beg your pardon! I did not see—. (*Hurries to* CHRISTENSEN.) Excuse me, but are you really comfortable in that chair?

Christensen. Thank you, I am just as uncomfortable here as anywhere else. It is the sitting down and getting up again that bothers me more than anything else. (*Looks round.*) I have just been to see him.

Riis. Hoff?

Christensen. Honest fellow. Stupid.

Riis. So long as he holds his tongue—

Christensen. He'll do that.

Riis. Thank heaven for that! Then we have only ourselves to consider. I suppose it cost you a bit?

Christensen. Not a penny!

Riis. You got out of it cheap, then.

Christensen. Yes, didn't I? Still, as a matter of fact, he has cost me quite enough already—although he knows nothing about that.

Riis. Indeed? When he failed, I suppose.

Christensen. No, when he married.

Riis. Oh, I understand.

Christensen. And I didn't think I should hear any more about it after that.—You ladies seem to be having a fine game of whispering! (MRS. CHRISTENSEN *comes forward.* RIIS *places chairs for her and his wife.*)

Mrs. Christensen. I was telling Mrs. Riis about the Miss Tang affair. She really seems to have risen from her grave!

Christensen. Is your daughter at home, may I ask?

Riis. I have sent to fetch her.

Mrs. Christensen. I hope the last few days have taught her a lesson too, poor girl! She suffers from a fault that unusually clever people are very liable to—I mean self-righteousness.

Riis. Exactly! You are perfectly right! But I should call it arrogance!

Mrs. Christensen. I should not like to say that—but presumption, perhaps.

Mrs. Riis. Why do you say that, Mrs. Christensen?

Mrs. Christensen. Because of various conversations I have had with her. I was speaking to her once about a man's being his wife's master. In these days it is a good thing to impress that on young girls.

Christensen. Yes, indeed!

Mrs. Christensen. And when I reminded her of certain words of St. Paul's, she said: "Yes, it is behind those bars that we women are still shut up." Then I knew that something would happen. Pride goes before a fall, you know.

Christensen. Oh, come, come! That won't do at all! Your chain of reasoning isn't sound!

Mrs. Christensen. How?

Christensen. It is not.　Because in the first place it was not Miss Riis that fell, but your precious son.　And in the second place his fall was not a consequence of Miss Riis's pride, because of course it happened many years before Miss Riis showed any of her pride.　So that if you knew that his fall would happen as a consequence of Miss Riis's pride, you knew something that you certainly did not know.

Mrs. Christensen. Oh, you are making fun of me!

Christensen. I ought to be at a committee meeting punctually at one.—May I ask what has become of your daughter?

Riis. Indeed I am really beginning to wonder— (*During the foregoing,* NORDAN *has remained in the background, sometimes in the room and sometimes outside in the park.* MARGIT *now goes past the window outside, and* NORDAN *is heard speaking to her.*)

Nordan. Have you only just found her?

Margit. No, sir—I have been down once already to take Miss Riis her hat, gloves and parasol.

Nordan. Is she going out?

Margit. I don't know, sir.　(*Goes out.*)

Christensen. Dear me!

Riis. What does it mean?　(*Turns to go and fetch her.*)

Nordan. No, no!　Do not you go!

Mrs. Riis. I expect I had better go—

Riis. Yes, you go!

Nordan. No, I will go.　I am afraid I am responsible for—.　(*As he goes*) I'll answer for it I will bring her back!

Christensen. Dear me!

Mrs. Christensen (*getting up*). I am afraid, my dear Mrs. Riis, we have come at an inconvenient time for your daughter?

Riis. Ah, you must be lenient with her! I assure you it is these high-flown ideas—this reading, that her mother has not been nearly firm enough in keeping her from.

Mrs. Riis. I? What are you talking about?

Riis. I say that this is a very important moment! And at moments like this one sees very clearly, very—well, that is what happens!

Christensen. Your husband, Mrs. Riis, has suddenly had the same sort of revelation as our parson had lately— I should say, my wife's parson. It was one day just after dinner—after an extremely good dinner, by the way—a moment when a man often has very bright ideas. We were talking about all the things a woman has to learn now, as compared with the old days, and how some people say it is mere waste of time because she will forget it all again when she marries. " Yes," said parson, looking very pleased, " my wife has completely forgotten how to spell; I hope she will soon forget how to write, too! "

Mrs. Christensen. You imitate people so well, that one cannot help laughing—although it isn't right. (CHRISTENSEN *looks at his watch.*)

Riis. It doesn't look as if they were coming back!— Will you go, or shall I?

Mrs. Riis (getting up). I will go. But you could not expect them already—

Riis (coming close up to her and speaking in an undertone). This is your doing! I see it clearly!

Mrs. Riis. I do not think you know what you are saying. (*Goes out.*)

Riis (coming forward). I really must apologise most humbly! It is the last thing I should ever have expected of Svava—because I pride myself that the obligations of courtesy have never been disregarded in my house before.

Mrs. Christensen. Perhaps something has happened?

Riis. I beg your pardon?—Good heavens!

Mrs. Christensen. Oh, do not misunderstand me! I only mean that young girls are so easily agitated, and then they do not like to show themselves.

Riis. All the same, Mrs. Christensen, all the same! At such a moment as this, too!—You really must excuse me, I shall have no peace till I find out for myself what has happened! (*Hurries out.*)

Christensen. If Alfred had been here, I suppose he would have been running about all over the park after these females, too.

Mrs. Christensen. Really, my dear!

Christensen. Aren't we alone?

Mrs. Christensen. Yes, but still—!

Christensen. Well, I say, as a certain famous man said before me: "What the devil was he doing in that galley?"

Mrs. Christensen. Do have a moment's patience! It is really necessary.

Christensen. Bah! Necessary! Riis is more afraid of a rupture than any of us. Did you see him just now?

Mrs. Christensen. Yes, of course I did, but—

Christensen. She has already gone much farther than she has any right to.

Mrs. Christensen. So Alfred thinks, too.

Christensen. Then he should have been here now, to say so. I asked him to come.

Mrs. Christensen. He is in love, and that makes a man a little timid.

Christensen. Nonsense!

Mrs. Christensen. Oh, that passes off when one is in love as often as you are. (*Gets up.*) Here they come!— No, not Svava.

L

Christensen. Is she not with them?

Mrs. Christensen. I don't see her.

Riis (appearing at the door). Here they are!

Mrs. Christensen. And your daughter too?

Riis. Yes, Svava too. She asked the others to go on ahead of her. I expect she wanted to collect herself a little.

Mrs. Christensen (sitting down again). Ah, you see, it was just what I thought, poor child!

Mrs. Riis (coming in). She will be here in a moment! (*Goes up to* Mrs. Christensen.) You must forgive her, Mrs. Christensen; she has had a bad time of it.

Mrs. Christensen. Bless my soul, of course I understand that! The first time one has an experience of this kind, it tells on one.

Christensen. This is positively beginning to get amusing!

Enter Nordan.

Nordan. Here we are! She asked me to come on a little ahead of her.

Riis. She is not going to keep us waiting any longer, I hope?

Nordan. She was just behind me.

Riis. Here she is! (*Goes to the door to meet her;* Nordan *and* Mrs. Riis *do the same from the other side of the room.*)

Christensen. One would think she were the Queen of Sheba.

(Svava *comes in, wearing her hat, and with her gloves and parasol in her hand.* Christensen *and* Mrs. Christensen *get up from their seats. She bows slightly to them, and comes to the front of the stage on the right-hand side. All sit down in silence.* Nordan *is at the extreme left, then* Mrs. Riis, Mrs.

CHRISTENSEN *and* CHRISTENSEN. *At the extreme right, but a little behind the others, is* RIIS, *who is sitting down one minute and standing the next.*)

Mrs. Christensen. My dear Svava, we have come here to—well, you know what we have come for. What has happened has distressed us very much; but what is done cannot be undone. None of us can excuse Alfred. But all the same we think that he might be granted forgiveness, especially at the hands of one who must know that he loves her, and loves her sincerely. That makes it a different matter altogether, of course.

Christensen. Of course!

Riis. Of course!

Nordan. Of course!

Mrs. Christensen. And, even if you don't quite agree with me about that, I hope you will agree with me about Alfred himself. I mean to say, that we consider his character, my dear Svava, should vouch to you for his fidelity. I know that, if you require it, he will give you his word of honour that—

Mrs. Riis (*getting up*). No! No!

Mrs. Christensen. What is the matter, my dear Mrs. Riis?

Mrs. Riis. No words of honour! He has to take an oath when he marries, anyway.

Nordan. But surely two make it all the safer, Mrs. Riis?

Mrs. Riis. No, no! No oath! (*Sits down again.*)

Christensen. I was struck with our friend Dr. Nordan's remark. Tell me, my dear sir, do you also take it for granted that the sort of thing my son has done ought to be an absolute bar to marriage with an honourable woman?

Nordan. Quite the contrary! I am quite sure it never

prevents any one getting married—and remarkably well married. It is only Svava that is behaving in an extraordinary manner in every respect.

Mrs. Christensen. I would not go so far as to say that; but there is one thing that Svava has overlooked. She is acting as if she were free. But she is not by any means free. A betrothal is equivalent to a marriage; at any rate, I am old-fashioned enough to consider it so. And the man to whom I have given my hand is thereby made my master and given authority over me, and I owe to him—as to a superior authority—my respect, whether he act well or ill. I cannot give him notice, or run away from him.

Riis. That is old-fashioned and sensible. I thank you heartily, Mrs. Christensen!

Nordan. And I too!

Mrs. Riis. But if it is too late after the betrothal—. (*Checks herself.*)

Mrs. Christensen. What do you mean, dear Mrs. Riis?

Mrs. Riis. Oh, nothing—nothing at all.

Nordan. Mrs. Riis means that if it is too late after the betrothal, why do people not speak out before they are betrothed?

Riis. What a thing to say!

Christensen. Well, it wouldn't be such a bad thing, would it? I imagine proposals in future being worded somewhat in this way: " My dear Miss So-and-So, up to date I have had such and such a number of love affairs— that is to say, so many big ones and so many little ones." Don't you think it would be a capital way to lead the conversation on to—

Nordan. —to assuring her that she is the only one you have ever loved?

Christensen. Well, not exactly that, but—

Riis. Here comes Alfred!

Mrs. Riis. Alfred?

Mrs. Christensen. Yes, it really is he!

Riis (who has gone to the door to meet ALFRED). Ah, that is right! We are so glad you have come!

Christensen. Well, my boy?

Alfred. When it came to the point, I could not do anything else—I had to come here.

Christensen. I quite agree with you.

Riis. Yes, it was only the natural thing to do. (ALFRED *comes forward and bows respectfully to* SVAVA. *She bows slightly, but without looking at him. He steps back again.*)

Nordan. Good morning, my boy!

Alfred. Perhaps I have come at an inconvenient moment.

Riis. Not a bit of it! Quite the contrary!

Alfred. At the same time, it seems evident to me that my presence is not welcome to Miss Riis. (*No one answers him.*)

Mrs. Christensen. But it is a family council we are holding—isn't it, my dear girl?

Riis. I assure you, you *are* welcome! And we are all particularly anxious to hear what you have to say!

Christensen. That is so.

Alfred. I have not succeeded in getting a hearing yet, you know. I have been refused admittance repeatedly—both in person and when I wrote. So I thought that if I came now, perhaps I should get a hearing.

Riis. Of course. Who can object to that?

Nordan. You shall have your hearing.

Alfred. Perhaps I may take Miss Riis's silence to mean

permission? In that case—well—it is nothing so very much that I have to say, either. It is merely to remind you that, when I asked for Miss Riis's hand, it was because I loved her with all my heart—her and no one else. I could not imagine any greater happiness, and any greater honour, than to be loved by her in return. And so I think still. (*He pauses, as if he expected an answer. They all look at* SVAVA.) What explanation I could have given of my own free will—indeed what explanation, under other circumstances, I should have felt impelled to give—I shall say nothing about now. But I *owe* no explanation! My honour demands that I should make a point of that. It is my future that I owe to her. And with regard to that I must confess I have been hurt— deeply hurt—by the fact that Miss Riis could doubt me for a moment. Never in my life has any one doubted me before. With all respect, I must insist that my word shall be taken. (*They are all silent.*) That is all I have to say.

Mrs. Riis (*getting up unwillingly*). But, Alfred, suppose a woman, under the same circumstances, had come and said the same thing—who would believe her? (*They are all silent.* SVAVA *bursts into tears.*)

Mrs. Christensen. Poor child!

Riis. Believe her?

Mrs. Riis. Yes, believe her. Believe her if, after a past like that, she came and assured us that she would make an honest wife?

Christensen. After a past like that?

Mrs. Riis. Perhaps that is putting it too harshly. But why should you require her to believe a man any more readily than a man would believe her? Because he would not believe her for a moment.

Riis (*coming up behind her*). Are you absolutely mad?

Christensen (half rising). Excuse me, ladies and gentlemen; the two young people must settle the affair now! *(Sits down again.)*

Alfred. I must confess I have never thought of what Mrs. Riis has just said, because such a thing never could happen. No man of honour would choose a woman of whose past he was not certain. Never!

Mrs. Riis. But what about a woman of honour, Alfred?

Alfred. Ah, that is quite different.

Nordan. To put it precisely: a woman owes a man both her past and her future; a man owes a woman only his future.

Alfred. Well, if you like to put it that way—yes.

Nordan (to Svava, *as he gets up).* I wanted you to postpone your answer, my child. But now I think you ought to answer at once. *(*Svava *goes up to* Alfred, *flings her glove in his face, and goes straight into her room.* Alfred *turns and looks after her.* Riis *disappears into his room on the right. Every one has risen from their seats.* Mrs. Christensen *takes* Alfred *by the arm and goes out with him;* Christensen *follows them.* Mrs. Riis *is standing at the door of the room which* Svava *has locked after her.)*

Nordan. That was throwing down a gauntlet, if you like!

Mrs. Riis (calling through the door). Svava!

Christensen (coming in and speaking to Nordan, *who has taken no notice of him and has not turned round).* Then it is to be war?—Well, I fancy I know a thing or two about war. *(Goes out.* Nordan *turns round and stands looking after him.)*

Mrs. Riis (still at the door). Svava! *(*Riis *comes rushing out of his room, with his hat on and his gloves and stick in his hand, and follows the* Christensens.*)* Svava!

ACT III

Scene I

(SCENE.—DR. NORDAN'S *garden, behind his neat one-storied house. He is sitting on a chair in the foreground, reading. His old servant,* THOMAS, *opens the house door and looks out.*)

Thomas. Doctor!

Nordan. What is it? (ALFRED *comes into sight in the doorway.*) Oh, it is you! (*Gets up.*) Well, my boy? You don't look up to much!

Alfred. No, but never mind that. Can you give me a bit of breakfast?

Nordan. Have you had no breakfast yet? Have you not been home then?—not been home all night?—not since yesterday? (*Calls*) Thomas!

Alfred. And when I have had something to eat, may I have a talk with you?

Nordan. Of course, my dear boy. (*To* THOMAS, *who has come out of the house*) Get some breakfast laid in that room, please (*pointing to a window on the left*).

Alfred. And may I have a wash too?

Nordan. Go with Thomas. I will be with you directly. (ALFRED *and* THOMAS *go into the house. Then a carriage is heard stopping outside.*) There is a carriage. Go and see who it is, Thomas. I won't see any patients! I am going away to-morrow.

Thomas. It is Mr. Christensen. (*Goes into the house again.*)

Nordan. Oho! (*Goes to the window on the left.*) Alfred!

Alfred (*coming to the window*). Yes?

Nordan. It is your father! If you do not want to be seen, pull down the blind. (*The blind is pulled down.*)

Thomas (*showing in* CHRISTENSEN). Will you come this way please, sir. (CHRISTENSEN *is in court dress protected by a dustcoat, and wears the cross of a Knight Commander of the Order of St. Olaf.*)

Christensen. I hope I do not disturb you, doctor?

Nordan. Not at all!—In full dress! I congratulate you.

Christensen. Yes, we newly-fledged knights have to go to Court to-day. But do you mind if I spend a minute or two here with you before I go on to the palace?—Any news from over there? From the Riis's?

Nordan. No. They are sitting waiting for the " war " to begin, I expect.

Christensen. They shall not have to wait long, then! I have made up my mind to begin it to-day. Has she come to her senses, by any chance? Women usually feel things like that very acutely. But they usually get over it, too.

Nordan. I do not think so. But I bow before your experience.

Christensen. Thank you! I should think that, as an old hand at playing the buffer in family jars, you had a much greater experience. Yesterday she was like an electric eel! And she gave her shock, too! The boy has not been home since. I am almost glad of that; it shows he has some sense of shame. I was beginning to doubt it.

Nordan. It is the coming " war " that interests me.

Christensen. Oh, you are anxious to see that, are you? Very well. As a matter of fact there is no need to draw up a plan of campaign. That affair of Mrs. North's can be taken up again any day, my dear fellow! It is in the hands of the bank, you know.

Nordan. But what has that to do with your son's engagement?

Christensen. What has it to do with it? Miss Riis gives my son his dismissal because she cannot tolerate his conduct before marriage. Her own father indulges in the same sort of conduct when he is well on in married life! *Tableau vivant très curieux !*—to use a language Mr. Riis is very fond of.

Nordan. It is a shame to talk like that—because your son is the only one to blame in this matter.

Christensen. My son is not in the least to blame in the matter! He has not done the slightest thing that could harm or discredit the Riis's—not the slightest thing! He is a man of honour, who has given Miss Riis his promise, and has kept it. Will any one dare to contradict that? Or to suggest that he will not keep his promise? If any one doubts him, it is an insult. Dr. Nordan! In this matter the alternatives are either an apology and peace—or war. For I am not going to put up with this sort of thing; and if my son puts up with it, I shall despise him.

Nordan. Oh, I quite believe your son had every honourable intention when he gave his promise. And very likely he would have kept it, too; I cannot say for certain, because I have learnt to doubt. I am a doctor—I have seen too much—and he did not appear to great advantage yesterday. You really must forgive my saying so—but after the liveliness of his young days, coupled with the tendencies he has inherited, do you think he really had any right to be surprised if people doubted him?—if his *fiancée* doubted him? Had he really any right to feel insulted, or to demand apologies? Apologies for what? For having doubted his virtue?—Just consider that!

Christensen. Why, what—?

Nordan. One moment! I was only half done. You said something about a reconciliation, you know; of course by that you meant a marriage. If your son is willing to marry a woman who distrusts him, then I shall despise him.

Christensen. Really—!

Nordan. Yes, indeed I shall. Our opinions are as different as all that. To my way of thinking, your son's only course is to submit—and wait; to keep silence, and wait—always supposing, of course, that he still loves her. That is my view of it.

Christensen. Well, I imagine that there are very few candidates for matrimony who have not been guilty of what my son has been guilty of; indeed, I am sure of it. And I imagine, too, that they have the same unfortunate " hereditary tendencies "—an expression on which you laid stress out of special friendship for me. But is that any reason why girls who are betrothed should behave as Miss Riis has been doing?—scream, and run away, and create a scandal? We should not be able to hear ourselves speak! It would be the queerest sort of anarchy the world has ever seen! Why, such doctrines as that are contrary to the very nature and order of things! They are mad! And when, into the bargain, they are thrown at our heads as if they were decisions of a High Court of Morality — well, then I strike! Good - bye! (*Starts to go, but turns back.*) And who is it that these High Court of Morality's decisions would for the most part affect, do you suppose? Just the ablest and most vigorous of our young men. Are we going to turn them out and make a separate despised caste of them? And what things would be affected, do you suppose? A great part of the world's literature and art; a great part of all that is loveliest and most captivating in the life of to-day; the world's greatest cities, most particularly—those wonders of the world—teeming with their millions of people! Let me tell you this: the life that disregards marriage or loosens the bonds of marriage, or transforms the whole institution—you know very well what I mean—the life that is accused of using the "weapons of seduction" in its fashions, its luxury, its entertainments, its art, its theatre—that life is one of the most potent factors in these teeming cities, one of the most fruitful sources of their existence! No one who has seen it can have any doubt about it, however ingenuous he may pretend to be. Are we to wish to play havoc with all that too?—to disown the flower of the world's youth, and ruin the world's finest cities? It seems to me that people wish to do so much in the name of morality, that they end by wishing to do what would be subversive of all morality.

Nordan. You are certainly embarking on your little war in the true statesmanlike spirit!

Christensen. It is nothing but sound common-sense, my dear sir; that is all that is necessary, I am sure. I shall have the whole town on my side, you may be certain of that!

Thomas (appearing at the house door). Doctor!

Nordan (turning round). Is it possible! *(Hurries to the doorway, in which* MRS. RIIS *appears.)*

Mrs. Riis. May I—?

Nordan. Of course! Will you come out here?

Mrs. Riis (to CHRISTENSEN, *who bows to her).* My visit is really to you, Mr. Christensen.

Christensen. I am honoured.

Mrs. Riis. I happened to look out into the street just

as your carriage stopped and you got out. So I thought I would seize the opportunity—because you threatened us yesterday, you know. Is that not so? You declared war against us?

Christensen. My recollection of it is that war was declared, Mrs. Riis, but that I merely accepted the challenge.

Mrs. Riis. And what line is your campaign going to take, if I may ask the question?

Christensen. I have just had the honour of explaining my position to the doctor. I do not know whether it would be gallant to do as much to you.

Nordan. I will do it, then. The campaign will be directed against your husband. Mr. Christensen takes the offensive.

Mrs. Riis. Naturally!—because you know you can strike at him. But I have come to ask you to think better of it.

Christensen (with a laugh). Really?

Mrs. Riis. Once—many years ago now—I took my child in my arms and threatened to leave my husband. Thereupon he mentioned the name of another man, and shielded himself behind that—for it was a distinguished name. " See how lenient that man's wife is," he said. " And, because she is so, all her friends are lenient, and that will be all the better for their child." Those were his words.

Christensen. Well, as far as the advice they implied was concerned, it was good advice—and no doubt you followed it.

Mrs. Riis. The position of a divorced woman is a very humiliating one in the eyes of the world, and the daughter of such a woman fares very little better. The rich and distinguished folk who lead the fashion take care of that.

Christensen. But what—?

Mrs. Riis. That is my excuse for not having the courage to leave him. I was thinking of my child's future. But it is my husband's excuse, too; because he is one of those who follows the example of others.

Christensen. We all do that, Mrs. Riis.

Mrs. Riis. But it is the leaders of society that set the example, for the most part; and in this matter they set a tempting one. I suppose I can hardly be mistaken in thinking that I have heard your view of this matter, all along, through my husband's mouth? Or, if I am mistaken in that, I at all events surely heard it more accurately yesterday, when I heard your voice in everything that your son said?

Christensen. I stand by every word of what my son said.

Mrs. Riis. I thought so. This campaign of yours will really be a remarkable one! I see your influence in everything that has happened, from first to last. You are the moving spirit of the whole campaign—on both sides!

Nordan. Before you answer, Christensen—may I ask you, Mrs. Riis, to consider whether you want to make the breach hopelessly irreparable? Do you mean to make a reconciliation between the young people quite impossible?

Mrs. Riis. It *is* impossible, as it is.

Nordan. Why?

Mrs. Riis. Because all confidence is destroyed.

Nordan. More so now than before?

Mrs. Riis. Yes. I will confess that up to the moment when Alfred's word of honour was offered yesterday—up to the moment when he demanded that his word of honour should be believed—I did not recognise the fact that it was my own story over again. But it was—word for word my own story! That was just the way we began; who will vouch for it that the sequel would not be the same as in our case?

Christensen. My son's character will vouch for that, Mrs. Riis!

Mrs. Riis. Character? A nice sort of character a man is likely to develop who indulges in secret and illicit courses from his boyhood! That is the very way faithlessness is bred. If any one wants to know the reason why character is such a rare thing, I think they will find the answer in that.

Christensen. A man's youth is by no means the test of his life. That depends on his marriage.

Mrs. Riis. And why should a man's faithlessness disappear when he is married? Can you tell me that?

Christensen. Because then he loves, of course.

Mrs. Riis. Because he loves? But do you mean that he has not loved before then? How absolutely you men have blinded yourselves!—No, love is not the least likely to be lasting when the will is vitiated. And that is what it is—vitiated by the life a bachelor leads.

Christensen. And yet I know plenty of sensual men who have strong wills.

Mrs. Riis. I am not speaking of strength of will, but of purity, faithfulness, nobility of will.

Christensen. Well, if my son is to be judged by any such nonsensical standard as that, I am devoutly thankful he has got out of the whole thing before it became serious—indeed I am! Now we have had enough of this. (*Prepares to go.*)

Mrs. Riis. As far as your son is concerned—. (*Turns to* NORDAN.) Doctor, answer me this, so that his father may hear it before he goes. When you refused to go with us to the betrothal party, had you already heard something about Alfred Christensen? Was what you had heard of such a nature that you felt you could not trust him?

Nordan (after a moment's thought). Not altogether, certainly.

Mrs. Riis (to CHRISTENSEN). There, you hear!—But will you let me ask you this, doctor: why did you not say so? Good God, why did you not speak?

Nordan. Listen to me, Mrs. Riis. When two young people, who after all are suited to one another—for they are that, are they not?

Christensen. They are that, I admit.

Nordan. When all of a sudden they fall madly in love with one another, what are you to do?

Christensen. Oh, rake up all sorts of stories and exaggerations—create a scandal!

Nordan. Indeed, I must confess—what as a matter of fact I have said—that I have become accustomed to things not being exactly as they should be in that respect. I looked upon these young people's engagement in the same light as I have looked on others—on most others—that is to say, as a lottery. It might turn out well; on the other hand it might turn out very badly.

Mrs. Riis. And you were willing to risk my daughter, whom you are so fond of—for I know you are fond of her —in a lottery? Could one possibly have a clearer proof of the real state of things?

Nordan. Yes, certainly! You yourself, Mrs. Riis— what did you do?

Mrs. Riis. I—?

Christensen. Bravo!

Nordan. You knew what Hoff had said—and more too. (CHRISTENSEN *laughs quietly.*) Nevertheless you helped your husband, if not actually to try and get her to overlook it, at all events to smooth things over.

Christensen. Bravo!

Nordan. And you called in my help to induce her to take time to think it over.

Christensen. Mothers observe a considerable difference between theory and practice in these matters, I notice.

Nordan. It was only when I saw how deeply it affected Svava—what a horror she had of it—that my eyes were opened. And the longer I listened to her, the more sympathy I felt for her; for I was young myself once—and loved. But that was such a long time ago—and I have grown tired—

Mrs. Riis (*who has sat down at the little table*). My God!

Nordan. Yes, Mrs. Riis. Let me tell you candidly—it is the mothers, and no one else, that by degrees have made me callous. Mothers look upon the whole thing so callously. The fact is that as a rule they know what is what.

Christensen. That they do, the dear creatures! And Mrs. Riis is no exception to the rule. You must admit, my dear madam, that you did all you could to hold on to a young man who had had a lively past? Not to mention the fact that this same young man had an extremely good social position—a thing I only allude to incidentally.

Nordan. Exactly. Rather than not give their daughters a prospect of what they call "a good marriage" they straightway forget all that they have suffered themselves.

Mrs. Riis. You see, we do not know that it will turn out the same in their case.

Nordan. You don't know it?

Mrs. Riis. No, I tell you that I did not think so! We believe that the man our daughter is going to marry is so much better. We believe that in their case there are stronger guarantees—that the circumstances are altogether different. It is so! It is a kind of illusion that takes hold of us.

Christensen. When there is a prospect of a good marriage, yes! I entirely agree with you, Mrs. Riis—for the first time. Moreover, I think there is another side to it. Isn't it possible that women have not suffered so much after all from the fact that men are men? What? I fancy the suffering has been more acute than serious—something like sea-sickness; when it is over—well, it is over. And so when it is the daughters' turn to go on board, the dear mothers think: "Oh, they will be able to get over it too! Only let us get them off!" For they are so anxious to get them off, that is the truth!

Mrs. Riis (*getting up and coming forward*). Well, if it is so, surely it is nothing to make fun of! It only shows what a woman can sink to, from living with a man.

Christensen Indeed!

Mrs. Riis. Yes—because each generation of women is endowed with a stronger and stronger aspiration for a pure life. It results unconsciously from the maternal instinct, and is intended as a protection for the defenceless. Even worthless mothers feel that. But if they succumb in spite of it, and each generation of married women in its turn sinks as deep as you say, the reason of it can only be the privilege that men enjoy as part of their education.

Christensen. What privilege?

Mrs. Riis. That of living as they please when they are bachelors, and then having their word of honour believed in when they choose to enter the married state. As long as women are powerless to put an end to that horrible privilege or to make themselves independent of it, so long will one half of the world continue to be sacrificed on account of the other half—on account of the other half's lack of self-control. That one privilege turns out to be

more powerful than all the striving for liberty in the
world. And that is not a laughing matter.

Christensen. You are picturing to yourself a different
world from this, and different natures from ours, Mrs.
Riis. And that—if you will excuse my saying so—is
obviously all the answer that is necessary to what you say.

Mrs. Riis. Well, then, give that answer openly! Why
do you not openly acknowledge that as your standpoint?

Christensen. But don't we?

Mrs. Riis. No—not here, at all events. On the contrary, you range yourselves ostensibly under our banner,
while all the time you are secretly betraying it. Why
have you not the courage to unfurl your own? Let these
bachelor customs of yours be sanctioned as entirely
suitable—then we should be able to join issue with you.
And then every innocent bride would be able to know
what it is she is entering upon—and in what capacity.

Nordan. That would be simply nothing more or less
than abolishing marriage.

Mrs. Riis. Would not that be more honest, too? Because now it is only being corrupted, long before it begins.

Christensen. Oh, of course it is all the men's fault! It
is the fashion to say that now—it is part of the " struggle
for freedom." Down with man's authority, of course!

Mrs. Riis. The authority his bachelor life has won
for him!

Nordan. Ha, ha!

Mrs. Riis. Do not let us cover up the real issue with
phrases! Let us rather speak of the " desolate hearth "
that the poet writes of. Marriage laid in ruins is what he
means by that; and what is the cause of it? What is the
cause of the chilly, horrible commonplace of every-day
life—sensual, idle, brutish? I could paint it even more
vividly, but I will not. I will refrain, for instance, from

bringing up the subject of hereditary disease. Let the question be thrashed out openly! Then perhaps a fire will be kindled—and our consciences stirred! It must become the most momentous question in every home. That is what is needed!

Christensen. Our conversation has soared to such heights that it really seems quite an anti-climax for me to say that I must go to a " higher place "!—but you must excuse me all the same.

Mrs. Riis. I hope I have not delayed you?

Christensen. No, there is plenty of time. I am only longing fervently—you really must not be offended—to get away from here.

Mrs. Riis. To your—equals?

Christensen. What a remarkable thing that you should remind me of them! And, by the way, that reminds me that I am scarcely likely to meet you or your family in future.

Mrs. Riis. No. Our acquaintance with you is at an end.

Christensen. Thank God for that!—All I hope now is that I shall succeed in apportioning the ridicule with some degree of justice.

Mrs. Riis. You need only publish your autobiography!

Christensen. No—I think it should rather be your family principles, madam! They are really very quaint. And when I relate the manner in which they are put into practice by yourselves, I rather think that people will be quite sufficiently amused. To speak seriously for a moment—I mean to attack your husband's reputation in private and in public, until he quits the town. I am not the sort of man to accept a humiliation like this without returning the compliment. (*Turns to go.*)

Nordan. This is shocking!

Alfred (*appearing in the doorway of the house*). Father!

Christensen. You here?—How ill you look, my boy! Where have you been?

Alfred. I came here at the same time as you did, and have heard everything. Let me tell you this at once, that if you take another step against the Riis's, I shall go round and tell every one the reason why Miss Riis threw me over. I shall tell them exactly what it was. Oh, it is no use looking at me with that mocking expression! I shall do it—and at once, too.

Christensen. I think you may spare yourself the trouble. The gossip about a broken engagement will get all over the town quicker than you could spread it.

Nordan (going up to ALFRED). One word, my boy—do you still love her?

Alfred. Do you ask that because she has been unjust to me? Well, now I know quite well what led to it—and inevitably led to it. I understand now!

Christensen. And forgive her? Without anything more?

Alfred. I love her more than ever—whatever she thinks of me!

Christensen. Well, upon my word! What next, I should like to know? You claim your right to resume the *rôle* of lover, and leave us and other honest folk to put the best face we can on the muddle you have made! I suppose you are going across the road now to tell her how much you enjoyed yourself yesterday?—or to ask for a respite till to-morrow, to give you time to pass decently through a process of purification? May I ask where you are going to find it and what it is going to consist of?— Oh, don't look so melodramatic! If you can put up with what you got from Riis's girl yesterday and her mother to-day, surely you can put up with a little angry talk or a little chaff from your father. I have had to put up with the whole affair—the betrothal and the breaking it off as well! And then to be sprinkled with essence of morality into the bargain! Good Lord! I hope at least I shall not smell of it still when I get to the palace. (*Goes towards the house, but turns back at the door.*) You will find some money in the office to pay for a trip abroad. (*Exit.*)

Nordan. Does that mean banishment?

Alfred. Of course it does. (*Appears very much agitated.*)

Mrs. Riis. Doctor, you must come over to our house with me—and at once!

Nordan. How is she?

Mrs. Riis. I don't know.

Nordan. You don't know?

Mrs. Riis. She wanted to be alone yesterday. And to-day she went out early.

Nordan. Has anything happened, then?

Mrs. Riis. Yes. You told me yesterday that you had given her a hint about—her father.

Nordan. Well?

Mrs. Riis. And so I felt that it could not be concealed any longer.

Nordan. And you have—?

Mrs. Riis. I have written to her.

Nordan. Written?

Mrs. Riis. It seemed the easiest way—and we should escape talking about it. All yesterday afternoon and last night I was writing, and tearing it up, and writing again—writing—writing! It was not a long letter, when all was done, but it took it out of me.

Nordan. And has she had the letter?

Mrs. Riis. When she had had her breakfast this morning and gone out, I sent it after her. And now, my dear friend, I want to beg you to go and have a talk with her—then you can let me know when I may go to her. Because I am frightened! (*Hides her face in her hands.*)

Nordan. The moment you came I saw something serious had happened. You argued so vehemently, too. Well, matters have developed, and no mistake!

Mrs. Riis. You mustn't go away, doctor! Don't go away from her now!

Nordan. Oh, that is it, is it?—Thomas!

Enter THOMAS.

Thomas. Yes, sir.

Nordan. You need not pack my things.

Thomas. Not pack, sir?—Very good, sir. (*Gives the doctor his stick and goes to open the house door for them.*)

Nordan. Allow me, Mrs. Riis. (*Offers her his arm.*)

Alfred (*coming forward*). Mrs. Riis! May I speak to her?

Mrs. Riis. Speak to her? No, that is impossible.

Nordan. You heard, my boy, what she has to think about to-day.

Mrs. Riis. And if she would not speak to you before, it is not likely she will now.

Alfred. If she should ask to speak to me, will you tell her I am here? I shall stay here till she does.

Mrs. Riis. But what is the use of that?

Alfred. Well, that will be our affair. I know she wants to speak to me, just as much as I do to her. Only tell her I am here! That is all I ask. (*Goes away into the farther part of the garden.*)

Nordan. He does not know what he is talking about.

Mrs. Riis. Dear Dr. Nordan, let us go! I am so frightened.

Nordan. Not more than I am, I think.—So she knows it now, does she! (*They go out.*)

Scene II

(Scene.—*The same as in Acts I. and II. Svava comes into the room slowly and looks round ; then goes to the door and looks round outside the house, then comes in again. As she turns back, she sees* Nordan *standing in the doorway.*)

Svava. You!—Oh, Uncle Nordan! (*Sobs.*)

Nordan. My child! My dear child! Calm yourself!

Svava. But haven't you seen mother? She said she had gone across to see you.

Nordan. Yes, she is coming directly. But look here— suppose you and I go for a good long walk together, instead of talking to your mother or any one? A long quiet walk? Eh?

Svava. I can't.

Nordan. Why?

Svava. Because I must make an end of all this.

Nordan. What do you mean?

Svava (*without answering his question*). Uncle—?

Nordan. Yes?

Svava. Does Alfred know this?—Did he know it before?

Nordan. Yes.

Svava. Of course every one knew it except me. Oh, how I wish I could hide myself away from every one! I will, too. I see the real state of things now for the first time. I have been like a child trying to push a mountain away with its two hands—and they have all been standing round, laughing at me, of course. But let me speak to Alfred!

Nordan. To Alfred?

Svava. I behaved so wrongly yesterday. I ought never to have gone into the room—but you gave me no choice when you came to me. I went with you almost unconsciously.

Nordan. I suppose it was thinking of your father—of what I told you about him—that made you—

Svava. I did not understand all at once. But, when I was by myself, it all flashed across me—mother's strange uneasiness—father's threats about leaving the country—all sorts of expressions, and signs—lots and lots of things I had never understood and never even thought twice about! I chased them out of my mind, but back they came!—back and back again! It seemed to paralyse me. And when you took me by the arm and said: " Now you must go in! "—I hardly had strength to think. Everything seemed to be going round and round.

Nordan. Yes, I made a regular mess of it—both on that occasion and the time before.

Svava. No, it was all quite right—quite right! We certainly went a little off the lines, it is true. I must speak to Alfred; the matter must not rest as it is. But, except for that, it was all quite right. And now I have got to make an end of it all.

Nordan. What do you mean?

Svava. Where is mother?

Nordan. My dear girl, you ought not to try and do anything to-day. I should advise you not to speak to anybody. If you do—well, I don't know what may happen.

Svava. But I know.—Oh, it is no use talking to me like that! You think I am simply a bundle of nerves to-day. And it is quite true—I am. But if you try to thwart me it will only make me worse.

Nordan. I am not trying to thwart you at all. I only—

Svava. Yes, yes, I know.—Where is mother, then? And you must bring Alfred here. I cannot go to him, can I? Or do you think he has too much pride to come, after what happened yesterday? Oh, no, he is not like that! Tell him he must not be proud with one who is so humiliated. (*Bursts into tears.*)

Nordan. But do you think you are able for it?

Svava. You don't know how much I can stand! Anyway, I must get done with it all, quickly. It has lasted long enough.

Nordan. Then shall I ask your mother—?

Svava. Yes!—and will you ask Alfred?

Nordan. Presently, yes. And if you should—

Svava. No, there is no " if " about it!

Nordan. —if you should want me, I won't go away till you are " done with it all," as you say. (SVAVA *goes up to him and embraces him. He goes out. After a short pause* MRS. RIIS *comes in.*)

Mrs. Riis (*going to* SVAVA). My child! (*Stops.*)

Svava. No, mother, I cannot come near you. Besides, I am trembling all over. And you don't understand what it is? It has not dawned upon you that you cannot treat me like this?

Mrs. Riis. Treat you like this, Svava? What do you mean?

Svava. Good heavens, mother!—letting me live here day after day, year after year, without letting me know what I was living with? Allowing me to preach the strictest principles, from a house like ours? What will people say of us, now that everything will be known!

Mrs. Riis. Surely you would not have wished me to tell my child that—

Svava. Not while I was a child. But when I had grown up, yes—under any circumstances! I ought to have been allowed the choice whether I would live at home under such conditions or not! I ought to have been allowed to know what every one else knew—or what they may get to know at any moment.

Mrs. Riis. I have never looked at it in that light.

Svava. Never looked at it in that light? Mother!

Mrs. Riis. Never!—To shield you and have peace in our home while you were a child, and peace afterwards in your studies, your interests and your pleasures—for you are not like other girls, you know, Svava—to ensure this, I have been almost incredibly careful that no hint of this should come to your ears. I believed that to be my duty. You have no conception what I have stooped to—for your sake, my child.

Svava. But you had no right to do it, mother!

Mrs. Riis. No right?—

Svava. No! To degrade yourself for my sake was to degrade me too.

Mrs. Riis (with emotion). Oh, my God—!

Svava. I do not reproach you for anything, mother! I would not do that for the world—my dear mother! I am only so infinitely distressed and appalled at the thought of your having to go about carrying such a secret with you! Never able to be your real self with me for a moment! Always hiding something! And to have to listen to my praises of what so little deserved praise—to see me putting my faith in him, caressing him—oh, mother, mother!

Mrs. Riis. Yes, dear, I felt that myself—many and many a time. But I felt that I dared not tell you. It was wrong—so very wrong! I understand that now! But would you have had me leave him at once, as soon as I knew of it myself?

Svava. I cannot take upon myself to say. You decided

that for yourself. Each one must decide that for herself —according to the measure of her love and her strength. But when the thing went on after I was grown up—! Naturally that was why I made a second mistake. I had been brought up to make mistakes, you see. (Riis *is heard outside the window, humming a tune.*)

Mrs. Riis. Good heavens, there he is! (Riis *is seen passing the left-hand window. When he reaches the door, however, he stops and, with the words, "Oh, by the bye!" turns back and goes hurriedly out.*)

Mrs. Riis. You look quite changed, my child! Svava, you frighten me! Surely you are not going to—?

Svava. What is it that is in your mind, mother?

Mrs. Riis. The thought that, as I have endured so much for your sake, you might make up your mind to endure a little for mine.

Svava. A little of this? No, not for a moment!

Mrs. Riis. But what are you going to do?

Svava. Go away from here at once, of course.

Mrs. Riis (with a cry). Then I shall go with you!

Svava. You? Away from father?

Mrs. Riis. It has been for your sake that I have stayed with him. I won't stay here a day without you!—Ah, you don't *want* me with you!

Svava. Mother, dear—I must have time to accustom myself to the changed state of things. You have quite changed in my eyes too, you see. I have been mistaken in you, and I must get accustomed to that idea. I must be alone!—Oh, don't look so unhappy, dear!

Mrs. Riis. And this is the end of it all—this is the end of it!

Svava. I cannot act otherwise, dear. I must go away now to my Kindergartens and give up my life entirely to that work. I must, I must! If I cannot be alone there, I must go farther afield.

Mrs. Riis. This is the cruellest part of it all—the cruellest part! Listen, is that—? Yes, it is he. Do not say anything now! For my sake say nothing now; I cannot bear anything more on the top of this!—Try to be friendly to him! Svava—do you hear me! (RIIS *comes back, still humming a tune ; this time he has his overcoat over his arm.* SVAVA *comes hurriedly forward, and after a moment's hesitation sits down with her back half turned to him, and tries to busy herself with something.* RIIS *puts down his overcoat. He is in court dress and wears the Order of St. Olaf.*)

Riis. Good morning, ladies! Good morning!

Mrs. Riis. Good morning!

Riis. Here is the latest great piece of news for you: Who do you think drove me from the palace? Christensen!

Mrs. Riis. Really?

Riis. Yes! Our wrathful friend of yesterday! Yes! He and one of my fellow-directors. I was one of the first persons he greeted when he got to the palace. He introduced me to people, chatted with me—paid me the most marked attention!

Mrs. Riis. You don't mean it?

Riis. Consequently nothing really happened here yesterday! No gloves were thrown about at all, least of all in his eldest son's face! Christensen, the worthy knight of to-day's making, feels the necessity for peace! We ended by drinking a bottle of champagne at my brother's.

Mrs. Riis. How amusing!

Riis. Therefore, ladies—smiles, if you please! Nothing has happened here, absolutely nothing! We begin again with an absolutely clean slate, without a smear upon it!

Mrs. Riis. What a piece of luck!

Riis. Yes, isn't it! That rather violent outburst of

our daughter's has unburdened her mind and cleared the ideas in other people's heads. The general atmosphere is agreeably clear, not to say favourable.

Mrs. Riis. And what was it like at the palace?

Riis. Well, I can tell you this—when I looked round at our batch of new-fledged knights, it did not exactly impress me that it is virtue that is rewarded in this world of ours. However, we were all confronted with an alarmingly solemn document. It was about something we swore to preserve—I fancy it was the State—or perhaps the Church—I am really not sure, because I didn't read it. They all signed it!

Mrs. Riis. You, as well?

Riis. I, as well. Do you suppose I was going to be left out of such good company? Up at those exalted heights one obtains a happier and freer outlook upon life. We were all friends up there. People came up and congratulated me—and after a bit I wasn't sure whether it was on my daughter's account or on my own; and, what is more, I never knew I had so many friends in the town, let alone at Court! But in such brilliant company and such an atmosphere of praises and compliments and general amiability, one was not inclined to be particular! And there were only men present! You know—you ladies must excuse me—there is sometimes a peculiar charm in being only with men, especially on great occasions like that. Conversation becomes more pointed, more actual, more robust—and laughter more full of zest. Men seem to understand one another almost without the need of words.

Mrs. Riis. I suppose you are feeling very happy to-day, then?

Riis. I should think I am!—and I only wish every one were the same! I daresay life might be better than it is;

but, as I saw it under those circumstances from those exalted heights, it might also be much worse. And, as for us men—oh, well, we have our faults, no doubt, but we are very good company for all that. It would be a dull world without us, I am sure. Let us take life as it comes, my dear Svava! (*Comes nearer to her. She gets up.*) What is the matter? Are you still in a bad temper? —when you have had the pleasure of boxing his ears with your own gloves, before the whole family circle? What more can you reasonably ask of life? I should say you ought to have a good laugh over it!—Or is there something up? What? Come, what is the matter now?

Mrs. Riis. The fact is—

Riis. Well, the fact is—?

Mrs. Riis. The fact is that Alfred will be here in a moment.

Riis. Alfred here? In a moment? Hurrah! I quite understand! But why didn't you tell me so at once?

Mrs. Riis. You have talked the whole time since you came in.

Riis. I do believe I have!—Well, if you are going to take it seriously, my dear Svava, perhaps you will allow your " knightly " father to take it lightly? The whole thing amuses me so tremendously. I was put into good spirits to-day the moment I saw, from Christensen's face, that there was nothing in the wind. And so Alfred is coming here directly! Then I understand everything. Hurrah, once more! I assure you that is the best of all the good things that have happened to-day. I really think I must play a festal overture till he comes! (*Goes towards the piano, singing.*)

Mrs. Riis. No, no, dear! Do you hear? No, no! (Riis *plays on, without listening to her, till she goes up to him, and stops him, pointing to* Svava.)

Svava. Oh, let him play, mother—let him play! It is the innocent gaiety that I have admired since I was a child! (*Bursts into tears, but collects herself.*) How hateful! How horrible!

Riis. My dear child, you look as if you wanted to be throwing down gauntlets to-day too! Isn't that all done with?

Svava. No, indeed it is not!

Riis. You shall have the loan of my gloves, if you haven't—

Mrs. Riis. Oh, don't say those things to her!

Svava. Oh, yes, let him! Let him mock at us, mother dear! A man of his moral earnestness has the right to mock at us!

Riis. What are you talking about? Does it show a lack of moral earnestness not to be in love with old maids and sour-faced virtue?

Svava. Father, you are—

Mrs. Riis. No, Svava!

Riis. Oh, let her say what she wants! It is something quite new to see a well-brought-up girl throw her gloves in her *fiancé's* face and accusations in her father's! Especially when it is all done in the name of morality!

Svava. Don't talk about morality! Or go and talk to Mrs. North about it!

Riis. Mrs.— Mrs.—? What has she to do with—?

Svava. Be quiet! I know everything! You have—

Mrs. Riis. Svava!

Svava. Ah, yes—for mother's sake I won't go on. But, when I threw down my much discussed gauntlet yesterday, I knew about it then. That was why I did it! It was a protest against everything of the kind, against its beginning and its continuation, against him and against you!

I understood—then—your pious zeal in the matter, and the show of scandalised morality you allowed mother to be a witness of!

Mrs. Riis. Svava!

Svava. I understand now, for the first time, what your consideration, your politeness to mother—which I have so often admired—all meant! Your fun, your good temper, your care of your appearance!—Oh, I never can believe in anything any more! It is horrible, horrible!

Mrs. Riis. Svava, dear!

Svava. All life seems to have become unclean for me! My nearest and dearest all soiled and smirched! That is why, ever since yesterday, I have had the feeling of being an outcast; and that is what I am — an outcast from all that I prized and reverenced—and that without my having done the slightest thing to deserve it. Even so, it is not the pain of it that I feel most deeply; it is the humiliation, the shame. All that I have so often said must seem now to be nothing but empty words—all that I have done myself must seem of no account—and this without its being my fault! For it is your fault! I thought, too, that I knew something about life; but there was more for me to learn! I see that you wanted me to give way to such an extent that I should end by acquiescing in it. I understand now, for the first time, what your teaching meant—and the things that you invoked mother and heaven to witness. But it is of no use! I can tell you that it is about as much as one can stand, to have the thoughts I have had yesterday—last night—to-day. However, it is once and for all; after this, nothing can ever take me by surprise again. To think that any man could have the heart to let his child have such an experience!

Mrs. Riis. Svava—look at your father!

N

Svava. Yes—but if you think what I am saying now is hard, remember what I said to you before I knew this— no longer ago than yesterday morning. That will give you some idea of how I believed in you, father—and some idea of what I am feeling now! Oh!—

Riis. Svava!

Svava. You have ruined my home for me! Almost every other hour in it has been corrupted—and I cannot face a future like that.

Riis and Mrs. Riis (together). But, Svava—!

Svava. No, I cannot! My faith in you is destroyed— so that I can never think of this as a home again. It makes me feel as if I were merely living with you as a lodger—from yesterday onwards, merely a lodger in the house.

Riis. Don't say that! My child!

Svava. Yes, I am your child. It only needed you to say it like that, for me to feel it deeply. To think of all the experiences we two have had together—all the happy times we have had on our travels, in our amusements— and then to think that I can never look back on them again, never take them up again! That is why I cannot stay here.

Riis. You cannot stay here!

Svava. It would remind me of everything too painfully. I should see everything in a distorted light.

Mrs. Riis. But you will see that you cannot bear to go away, either!

Riis. But—*I* can go!

Mrs Riis. You?

Riis. Yes, and your mother and you stay here?—Oh, Svava—!

Svava. No, I cannot accept that—come what may!

Riis. Do not say any more! Svava, I entreat you!

Do not make me too utterly miserable! Remember that never, until to-day—I never thought to make you—. If you cannot bear to be with me any more—if you cannot— then let me go away! It is I that am to blame, I know. Listen, Svava! It must be I, not you! You must stay here!

Mrs. Riis (listening). Good heavens, there is Alfred!

Riis. Alfred! (*A pause.* ALFRED *appears in the door-way.*)

Alfred (after a moment). Perhaps I had better go away again?

Riis (to ALFRED). Go away again?—Go away again, did you say?—No, not on any account! No!—No, you could not have come at a more fortunate moment! My boy, my dear boy! Thank you!

Mrs. Riis (to SVAVA). Would you rather be alone—?

Svava. No, no, no!

Riis. You want to speak to Svava, don't you? I think it will be best for me to leave you together. You need to talk things over frankly with her—to be alone—naturally! You will excuse me, then, if I leave you, won't you? I have something very important to do in town, so you will excuse me! I must hurry and change my clothes—so please excuse me! (*Goes into his room.*)

Alfred. Oh, but I can come some other time.

Mrs. Riis. But I expect you would like to talk to her now?

Alfred. It is no question of what I would like. I see —and I heard Dr. Nordan say—that Miss Riis is quite worn out. But I felt it my duty, all the same, to call.

Svava. And I thank you for doing so! It is more— far more—than I have deserved. But I want to tell you at once that what happened yesterday—I mean, the form my behaviour took yesterday—was due to the fact that, only an hour before then, something had come to my knowledge that I had never known before. And that was mixed up with it. (*She can scarcely conceal her emotion.*)

Alfred. I knew that to-day you would be regretting what happened yesterday—you are so good. And that was my only hope of seeing you again.

Riis (*coming out of his room partly dressed to go out*). Does any one want anything done in town? If so, I shall be happy to see to it! It has occurred to me that perhaps these ladies would like to go away for a little trip somewhere—what do you two say to that? When one's thoughts are beginning to get a little—what shall I call it?—a little too much for one, or perhaps I should rather say a trifle too serious, it is often a wonderful diversion to go away for a little change. I have often found it so myself—often, I assure you! Just think it over, won't you? I could see about making plans for you at once, if you think so—eh? Well, then, good-bye for the present! And—think it over! I think myself it is such an excellent plan! (*Goes out.* SVAVA *looks at her mother with a smile, and hides her face in her hands.*)

Mrs. Riis. I must go away for a few minutes and—

Svava. Mother!

Mrs. Riis. I really must, dear! I must collect my thoughts. This has been too much for me. I shall not go farther away than into my room there (*pointing to the room on the left*). And I will come back directly. (SVAVA *throws herself into a chair by the table, overcome by her emotion.*)

Alfred. It looks as if we two were to have to settle this matter, after all.

Svava. Yes.

Alfred. I daresay that you will understand that since yesterday I have done nothing else but invent speeches to make to you—but now I do not feel as if it had been of much use.

Svava. It was good of you to come.

Alfred. But you must let me make one request of you, and that from my heart: Wait for me! Because I know now what will show me the way to your heart. We had planned out our life together, you and I; and, although I shall do it alone, I shall carry out our plans unfalteringly. And then perhaps, some day, when you see how faithful I have been—. I know I ought not to worry you, least of all to-day. But give me an answer! You need scarcely say anything—but just give me an answer!

Svava. But what for?

Alfred. I must have it to live on—and the more difficult the prize is to attain, the better worth living will life be to me. Give me an answer!

Svava (*tries to speak, but bursts into tears*). Ah, you see how everything upsets me to-day. I cannot. Besides, what do you want me to do? To wait? What would that mean? It would mean being ready and yet not ready; trying to forget and yet always having it before my mind. (*Is overcome again by her emotion.*) No!

Alfred. I see you need to be alone. But I cannot bring myself to go away. (Svava *gets up, and tries to regain control over herself.* Alfred *goes to her and throws himself on his knees beside her.*) Give me just one word.

Svava. But do you not understand that if you could give me back once more the happiness that complete trust gives—do you think I should wait for you to ask anything of me then? No, I should go to you and thank you on my knees. Can you doubt that for a moment?

Alfred. No, no!

Svava. But I have not got it.

Alfred. Svava!

Svava. Oh, please—!

Alfred. Good-bye—good-bye! But I shall see you again some day? I shall see you again? (*Turns to go, but stops at the door.*) I must have a sign—something definite to take with me! Stretch out a hand to me! (*At these words* SVAVA *turns to him and stretches out both her hands to him. He goes out.* MRS. RIIS *comes in from her room.*)

Mrs. Riis. Did you promise him anything?

Svava. I think so. (*Throws herself into her mother's arms.*)